Do Your Own Financial Planning

An Easy-to-Use Guide for Achieving Financial Security

Rob Flanigan

First Edition

Financial Sense
Madison, Wisconsin

A note to the reader . . .

In preparing this book, every effort was made to provide the most current, correct, and clearly expressed information possible. Nonetheless, inadvertent errors and omissions may be present. Also, inevitable changes in tax laws, government regulations, Social Security rules, available products and services, etc. will lessen the book's value with time.

This book offers general financial planning guidelines. Consequently, it should not substitute for more personalized legal, accounting, or tax advice. Readers are encouraged to consult with professional advisors for advice concerning specific matters before making any decision. The author and publisher disclaim any responsibility for positions taken by readers in their individual cases or for any misunderstanding on the part of readers.

First Printing 1997
Printed in the United States of America

Cover Design: Dave Kotwitz

Library of Congress Catalog Card Number: 96-96582

ISBN 0-9653316-0-1

Financial Sense
3818 Birch Avenue
Madison, WI 53711

Contents

Introduction 1

PART ONE: Develop Your Plan

SAVINGS

Retirement 4
College 12
Emergency 17

INSURANCE

Life 18
Short-Term Disability 21
Long-Term Disability 22
Health 27
Liability 29
Home 31
Auto 34

ESTATE PLANNING

Severe Disability 38
Death 39

Putting It All Together in a Budget 42
When To Update Your Financial Plan 45
Where To Get Help 47

PART TWO: Implement Your Plan

Your Income 50
Your Net Worth 51
Your Social Security Benefits 52
Retirement Savings — Estimating Your Needs 54
Life Insurance — Estimating Your Needs 59
Life Insurance — Shopping Instructions 76
Life Insurance — Managing Benefits 82
Disability Insurance — Shopping Instructions 85
Health Insurance — Shopping Instructions 90
Home, Auto, & Liability Insurance — Shopping Instructions 91
Insurance Company Ratings 98
Mutual Funds 99
Annuities 105

Index 107

To Mona

Special thanks to Dave Butler, Dorothea Custer, Pat Farrell, Mike Flanagan, Barbara Flanigan, David Flanigan, Elinor Flanigan, Mona Flanigan, Val Johnson, Dave Kotwitz, Ed Pierce, Joel Ungrodt, Lyn Ungrodt, Scott Wandschneider, and the helpful people at the Madison Public Library, the Janesville Public Library, and the University of Wisconsin – Madison Library.

Introduction

We had our first child . . . and suddenly we found our names on a whole new set of mailing lists. Among the expected advertisements for children's books, toys, and clothing, we also received information about financial products and services that would help us save for college and protect us from ruin. Like most people, we knew that our financial situation was dramatically different now that we had someone depending on us. We were also aware that financial goals are easiest to achieve when you start young. However, we were relatively uninformed about how to develop our financial plan, and we were skeptical of the intentions of sales agents who offered to help us.

In an effort to become more informed, I went to the library in search of practical advice. I wasn't sure at that time if I would be getting the background information necessary to make good use of a financial planner, or if I would be doing my own planning. What I found at the library did not make me happy. The books were thick with details, making them difficult to decipher let alone use to make decisions. I reluctantly began to pour over these books. During my studies, I gradually discovered that financial planning is not difficult. In fact, it's quite simple once you learn the basics. Thinking that others might benefit from my discovery, I took thorough notes. Now, after three years of research, training, and careful thought, I have completed my family's financial plan and this book.

□ The Book

Do Your Own Financial Planning explains the basics of financial planning and then adds recommendations, worksheets, and shopping instructions so you can make informed decisions and implement them efficiently. As you record your personal information in the book, please keep in mind that financial planning is not a science—the future is far too uncertain to justify numbers precise to the dollar. Use a pencil so you can easily make changes.

The book is divided into two parts:

Part One helps you develop your financial plan by stepping you through the planning topics, such as retirement savings, emergency savings, life insurance, and budgeting. It also explains *when* to update your plan and *where* you can get help if you need it.

Part Two provides supporting information for Part One. You are directed into Part Two as you develop your plan in Part One.

As you read, you will find many references to other pages of the book. Although this may be distracting, these references enhance the book's usefulness by keeping secondary details out of the information you need to make decisions.

This book serves married and single people during any stage of their lives. However, the book is specifically designed for people under age 50. Readers over 50 should seek additional guidance, especially in the areas of retirement savings and health insurance.

Throughout the book you will find space to record numbers for both you and a spouse. Obviously, if you are single you can ignore the requested spouse information. It is important for married people to be consistent regarding who is *you* and who is the *spouse*. Use the spaces below to note who is who.

You ____________ Spouse ____________

You will derive great satisfaction and save lots of money by doing your own financial planning. And even if you decide to get professional assistance with parts of your plan, this book will serve you well when communicating with these advisors and evaluating their suggestions.

As you begin to purchase financial products and speak with others about financial planning, you may find disagreement with certain suggestions presented in this book. Such disagreement is common. When I encountered opposing views in my research, I consulted books and practitioners until I found the advice I believed to represent the best interests of the consumer.

I hope you find this book useful. Happy Planning.

PART ONE

Develop Your Plan

RETIREMENT SAVINGS

How Much to Save 4
The Rule of Thumb 4
The Software 5
The Workbook 5
Where to Save 5
Employer Retirement Plans 6
Individual Retirement Accounts (IRAs) 8
Annuities 8
Cash-Value Life Insurance 9
Stock Mutual Funds 10

Will you live comfortably during retirement? Probably not, if you rely solely on employer savings and Social Security. Therefore, you should assess your need for added personal savings. **Don't wait!** A five year delay in your planning can raise your annual savings need by more than 50%.

☐ How Much to Save

Retirement planning has never been easier thanks to some new, inexpensive software and workbooks. The investment companies that offer these products do so in an effort to make it easier for you to save and potentially use their services. These planning tools are updated regularly to reflect rule changes and other current information. This book includes instructions for using two of the best products available. Ordering information appears on the next page.

To ensure that your planning efforts do not get stalled while you wait for the software or workbook to arrive, you may wish to begin planning with a simple rule of thumb.

The Rule of Thumb

A common rule of thumb suggests that you should save 10% of your income each year for retirement. This rule is known as The 10% Rule. To apply it, simply multiply your gross annual income by 0.1. Turn to page 50 for assistance in determining your gross income.

The 10% Rule is a helpful guide, but it should not substitute for the more accurate methods described next, because it does not account for important issues such as your specific personal retirement goals and your Social Security benefits.

The Software

If you have access to a personal computer, you should estimate your savings needs using specially designed software. Such software makes it easy to set goals and measure the impacts of changes in your goals, such as changing your retirement age.

One of the best products is Fidelity Investments' *Thinkware* for Windows or DOS. (A Macintosh version is not available.) The cost is roughly $20 after shipping. To obtain your copy, phone 800-457-1768. Ask the representative to review the computer requirements with you. When you receive the software, turn to page 54 of this book for special instructions.

The Workbook

If you do not have access to a personal computer, you may estimate your savings needs using a workbook. T. Rowe Price offers a free *Retirement Planning Kit.* You can request a copy by calling 800-541-4041. When you receive the workbook, turn to page 57 of this book for special instructions.

☐ Where to Save

Postponing taxes is the key to retirement investing because your money can accumulate more quickly. There are two ways to postpone taxes: tax-deductible contributions and tax-deferred growth. You want investments that accomplish both.

Best Places to Save . . .

- Employer Retirement Plans
- Individual Retirement Accounts (IRAs)

Both of these savings methods can offer tax-deductible contributions *and* tax-deferred growth. But both limit the amount you can save each year.

Other Places to Save . . .

- Annuities
- Cash-Value Life Insurance
- Stock Mutual Funds

None of these savings methods allow tax-deductible contributions. However, annuities and cash-value life insurance *do* provide tax-deferred growth, while stock mutual funds offer tax-deferral to the extent that some capital gains taxes are postponed until you sell.

An Estate Planning Consideration . . .

One goal of estate planning is to minimize taxes as you pass wealth to your heirs. So, if you are saving more money than you expect to need during your retirement, consider putting these extra savings in cash-value life insurance or stock mutual funds. Here's why. Upon your death, cash-value life insurance policies are *not* subject to income taxes (as are employer retirement plans, IRAs, and annuities), and stock mutual funds are *not* subject to capital gains taxes.

The following pages explain these investment choices and help you construct a savings plan.

Employer Retirement Plans

Most employer plans allow tax-deductible contributions *and* tax-deferred growth—making them the best places to save for retirement. Here are the names of some common employer plans:

401(k)s
403(b)s
Keoghs
Profit-Sharing
Pensions
Simplified Employee Pensions (SEPs)
Deferred Compensation
Tax-Sheltered Annuities (TSAs)[1]

Learn the plans available to you. If any of them **do not** permit tax-deductible contributions, do not use them until you reach the contribution limits on your other tax-deductible employer plans and your IRAs.

Does your employer match your contributions? For instance, your employer might pitch-in 50¢ for every $1 you contribute to your 401(k) plan. Take full advantage of this matching, even if you don't need the extra savings.

Many employer plans offer several investment alternatives. When you have a choice, select mutual funds that invest in growth stocks. Growth stocks have historically outperformed other types of investments (although there is no guarantee this performance will continue), and mutual funds are the practical way to invest. When you are ready to invest, refer to page 99 for more information about mutual funds.

If you leave your job, your employer may allow you to transfer your savings out of its retirement plan without penalty. (Or your employer might *require* you to transfer your savings.) You should move these savings into a **Rollover IRA** or into your new employer's retirement plan. A Rollover IRA is your best alternative unless your new employer gives you a special incentive to transfer your money into its plan. The Rollover IRA gives you complete control over your savings, while most employer plans limit your investment choices. Set up your Rollover IRA through a mutual fund company. Ask the mutual fund company to handle the transfer so you avoid potential tax penalties. Once this special IRA is established, **do not** make annual contributions to it as you would to a regular IRA. If you *do* make contributions (other than additional rollovers), you lose the ability to transfer this money into a future employer's retirement plan. There will probably never be a good reason to move your money out of the Rollover IRA, but you should leave the option open. Set up a regular IRA (discussed next) for your yearly IRA contributions.

---

[1] Tax-sheltered annuities may be offered to employees of charitable organizations and educational systems. They should not be confused with tax-deferred annuities, discussed under the heading *Annuities* on page 8.

RETIREMENT SAVINGS WORKSHEET

This table helps you and your spouse (denoted *you* and *sps*, respectively) decide where to make your retirement contributions.

A TOTAL CONTRIBUTION NEEDED (Year: ______) A __________
On line **A**, enter this year's total contribution estimated using the software or workbook (see page 5).

> NOTE: Your contribution should increase each year with the cost-of-living. To calculate each new year's contribution, multiply the previous year's amount by 1.04. This calculation assumes that the cost-of-living rises 4% per year.

B Employer's Defined Contribution B_{you} __________ B_{sps} __________
On line B_{you}, enter your employer's expected contribution to your retirement plan this year. (For a quick estimate, use last year's contribution.) Do the same for your spouse on line B_{sps}.

- If you have a pension plan where the annual contribution is not defined, do not try to estimate this contribution. You should have already accounted for this pension in the software or workbook.
- Do not include employer matching contributions—these are entered on line **D** below.
- Include only the vested portion of contributions, unless you expect to be fully vested by the time you leave your job.

Add the values on line **B** to see if you already exceed your savings needs shown on line **A**. In any event, you should complete lines **C** and **D** to take advantage of employer matching contributions.

C Your Voluntary Contribution to an C_{you} __________ C_{sps} __________
Employer Plan to Obtain Matching On line C_{you}, enter the amount *you* must contribute to your employer plans to get your employer's matching contributions. (For a quick estimate, use last year's value.) Do the same for your spouse on line C_{sps}.

D Employer's Matching Contribution D_{you} __________ D_{sps} __________
On line D_{you}, enter your employer's matching contribution. (For a quick estimate, use last year's value.) Do the same for your spouse on line D_{sps}.

Add the values on lines **B**, **C**, and **D** to see if you meet or exceed your savings needs shown on line **A**. If you have enough savings, you can skip the rest of this chapter. Otherwise, note the extra savings you need and continue to line **E**.

E Your Additional Voluntary E_{you} __________ E_{sps} __________
Contribution to an Employer Plan Your employer might allow you to make additional *tax-deductible* contributions up to some limit. Learn this limit from your benefits coordinator and enter the amount you plan to save on line E_{you}. (For a quick estimate, use last year's limit.) If no additional *tax-deductible* contributions are allowed, enter zero for now so you can first consider your spouse's retirement plan and both of your IRAs. Do the same for your spouse on line E_{sps}.

Add the values on lines **B**, **C**, **D**, and **E** to compare with your savings needs shown on line **A**. If you now have enough savings, you can skip the rest of this chapter. Otherwise, note the extra savings you need and read about Individual Retirement Accounts on the next page.

Individual Retirement Accounts (IRAs)

An IRA is your next best choice for retirement savings. Your savings grow tax-deferred, and your contributions *may* be tax-deductible (depending on your income and your participation in employer plans). IRAs strictly limit an individual's annual contribution to $2,000 or less. (Beginning in 1997, a non-working spouse may contribute the full $2,000 to an IRA.)

The best place for your IRA is with a mutual fund company. To begin an IRA, or to transfer money from an existing IRA, simply call a mutual fund company and request an IRA application. The application offers you three ways to make additional contributions. These methods are described below.

- **Payroll deduction** is the best way to contribute, but not all employers offer it. With payroll deduction, your employer makes your contributions and then deducts them from your paycheck. This method is effortless for you, and it assures that you will not forget to contribute.
- **Automatic withdrawal** should be your second choice. With automatic withdrawal, money is periodically transferred from one of your personal accounts, such as a checking account. This method is less convenient than payroll deduction because you must make sure your account stays above its minimum balance.
- **Personal check** is the least favorable alternative because it involves the discipline and inconvenience of writing and mailing monthly checks.

For maximum growth potential, select mutual funds that invest in growth stocks. When you are ready to invest, refer to page 99 for information about mutual funds.

RETIREMENT SAVINGS WORKSHEET

. . . continued

F Your Contribution to an IRA F*you* ___________ F*sps* ___________

On line **F***you*, enter the amount you plan to contribute to your personal IRA. Do the same for your spouse on line **F***sps*.

Add the values on lines **B**, **C**, **D**, **E**, and **F** to compare with your savings needs shown on line **A**. If you need more savings, note the amount, and either return to line **E** on the previous page (to make *taxable* contributions to an employer plan) or read about annuities, cash-value life insurance, and stock mutual funds.

Annuities

Annuities are tax-deferred savings plans sold by insurance companies.

Do not consider an annuity unless you are making the maximum allowed contributions to your employer retirement plans and IRAs, and still need more savings. Even then, don't consider an annuity unless you plan to keep your money in it for at least 15 or 20 years. This is how long it can take for the benefits of tax-deferral to overcome the added costs of an annuity.

If you want to consider an annuity, or if you have one you don't need, turn to page 105 for more information.

RETIREMENT SAVINGS WORKSHEET

. . . continued

G Your Contributions to Annuities **G** ___________

On line **G**, enter the total amount you and your spouse plan to contribute to annuities this year. Do not include contributions to annuities within employer retirement plans (such as tax-sheltered annuities) because these savings should have been listed on lines **C** and **E**.

Add the values on lines **B**, **C**, **D**, **E**, **F**, and **G** to compare with your savings needs shown on line **A**.

Cash-Value Life Insurance

Cash-value life insurance includes products such as *whole life*, *ordinary life*, *universal life*, *variable life*, *variable universal life*, *adjustable life*, *single-premium life*, and others similarly named. These products combine life insurance with a tax-deferred savings plan.

Do not consider cash-value life insurance unless you are making the maximum allowed contributions to your employer retirement plans and IRAs, and still need more savings. The following passages explain the basics of using cash-value life insurance for retirement savings.

With careful planning, cash-value life insurance *might* outperform an annuity. Here's how. When an annuity provides income during retirement, some of this income is taxed. A cash-value life policy can provide this same income—tax free. To do this, you simply borrow against the cash value of the policy in regular installments with no intention of repayment. This *income* you receive is not taxed because you are merely borrowing from your death benefit. To make this strategy work, you must select and use your policy carefully:

- Cash-value life insurance is typically more expensive than an annuity, so fewer of your dollars work for you. Make sure you fully understand the commissions, fees, and expenses. If the fees and expenses can vary during the life of the policy, determine the worst-case scenario using the policy's guaranteed rates, and investigate the company's track record for raising its rates. To be safe, only consider policies from insurance companies with superior ratings.
- Buy a policy with the lowest possible death benefit. (You *should not* include these death benefits in your life insurance plan.) This strategy keeps the policy's life insurance portion small relative to the investment portion, keeping expenses down. As your cash value increases, so will your death benefit. In fact, the law requires that your death benefit remain larger than your cash value so the policy still qualifies as life insurance. Otherwise it would become a pure investment vehicle with unique tax advantages.

- Make sure your policy does not levy special penalties for borrowing against your cash value (other than the usual interest charges).
- During retirement, keep track of how much cash value you can borrow. If you borrow too much, your policy will lapse and you must pay all of your deferred taxes.

If you want to consider a new or existing cash-value policy for retirement savings, seek the assistance of a knowledgeable fee-only financial planner. Page 47 will help you find such a planner.

RETIREMENT SAVINGS WORKSHEET

. . . continued

H Your Contributions to Cash-Value Life Insurance **H** ___________

If you own any cash-value life insurance purely as a retirement investment, enter on line **H** the portion of this year's premium that will go toward cash value. **Do not** include premiums for policies that are part of your life insurance plan.

Add the values on lines **B**, **C**, **D**, **E**, **F**, **G**, and **H** to compare with your savings needs shown on line **A**.

Stock Mutual Funds

The best way to save for retirement is to invest in stock mutual funds through employer retirement plans and IRAs. However, if you are making the maximum allowed contributions to these plans, and you still need more savings, consider investing some of this extra money in mutual funds outside of a tax-advantaged account. This strategy makes sense in the following situations:

- You want penalty-free access to this money before retirement.
- You want an investment with the estate planning advantage discussed on page 5.

To postpone the most taxes, choose a fund that emphasizes capital appreciation (instead of dividend income), and one that holds its stocks for a long time.

Set up your account with a mutual fund company that holds *none* of your other savings. This will prevent you from accidently spending this money.

Make your contributions using payroll deduction or automatic withdrawal (see page 8).

RETIREMENT SAVINGS WORKSHEET

. . . continued

I **Your Contributions to Stock Mutual Funds** I ___________

On line **I**, enter the total amount you and your spouse plan to invest this year toward retirement in stock mutual funds outside of tax-advantaged accounts.

Add the values on lines **B**, **C**, **D**, **E**, **F**, **G**, **H**, and **I** to compare with your savings needs shown on line **A**.

COLLEGE SAVINGS

How Much to Save 12
Where to Save
Stock Mutual Funds 13
State Education Bonds 14
Where NOT to Save
Series EE U.S. Savings Bonds 14
CollegeSure Certificates of Deposit 15
Prepaid Tuition Programs 16
Annuities 16
Cash-Value Life Insurance 16

The key to saving for college is starting early. The longer you wait to begin saving, the less manageable these savings become.

☐ How Much to Save

The worksheet on the next page will help you calculate college savings needs for your children. Before you fill it in, you must make a few decisions.

First, consider the type of schools, and therefore the cost of the schools, you expect your children to attend. If you don't have a specific school in mind, use one of the numbers listed in the table below. For information about a particular school, call the school, or ask your librarian to help you find a recent college guidebook (such as *The College Handbook* by the College Entrance Examination Board).

1997-98 COLLEGE COSTS

Type of School	Yearly Cost
2-year community college	$ 3,500
4-year public university	10,000
4-year private university	20,000

College costs will undoubtedly increase between now and the time your children enroll. To account for this rise, the worksheet assumes that your savings grow at the same rate as college costs. This assumption greatly simplifies the calculations, while providing a reasonable estimate of your savings needs.

You must also consider what percentage of your children's education you plan to fund through savings. Experts suggest that it is sufficient to save for 80% of college costs, because the remaining 20% can come from other sources, such as financial aid, student loans, your children's employment, or *your* income during the college years.

Once you have settled on some numbers, you can begin to fill in the worksheet. A sample calculation has been provided to assist you.

COLLEGE SAVINGS WORKSHEET

Child's name	Sample					
Yearly cost Portion of cost to save for	\$ 10,000 x 0.80	 x	 x	 x	 x	 x
Yearly cost to save for No. of years in college	8,000 x 4	 x	 x	 x	 x	 x
Total cost to save for Value of current savings	32,000 – 1,600	 –	 –	 –	 –	 –
Remaining cost to save for No. of years until college	30,400 ÷ 16	 ÷	 ÷	 ÷	 ÷	 ÷
Amount to save this year	\$ 1,900					

NOTE: Your contributions should increase each year to match the rise in college costs. To calculate the new year's contributions, multiply the previous year's amounts by 1.06. This calculation assumes that college costs grow 6% per year.

☐ Where to Save

No matter which of the following investments you choose, make saving easy and reliable using payroll deduction or automatic withdrawal (see page 8).

Stock Mutual Funds

Stock mutual funds offer the best way to save for college. Historically, stocks have outperformed other investment types over the long-term, even after taxes. (Although there is no guarantee this performance will continue.) Page 99 provides detailed information about mutual funds.

You can establish a mutual fund account in *your* name or *your child's* name.

- **When you use *your* name**, *you* maintain control of the money, and *you* pay taxes on the earnings at your income tax rate. **Here's a tax-saving tip:** When the time comes to pay college expenses, don't sell the mutual fund shares yourself, because you'll probably owe 28% tax on the fund's capital gains. Instead, transfer the shares into your child's name and have your child sell them. Your child will probably owe only 15% tax on the gains. (You and your spouse can each give up to $10,000 per year to each child without owing gift taxes.)
- **When you use *your child's* name**, you create a Uniform Gift-Transfer to Minor Account. Savings in this type of account can grow faster because all (or most) of the earnings are taxed at your child's income tax rate instead of yours. However, there are several drawbacks:

  (1) You cannot take back the money you contribute.

  (2) You must spend it on your child according to certain rules.

  (3) At age 18 or 21 (depending on your state—ask your banker) your child gains complete control of the account.

  (4) This money might weaken your child's ability to obtain financial aid.

  If you are interested in a Uniform Gift-Transfer to Minor Account, find an income tax guide at your library or bookstore for details. Also, find *Barron's Complete College Financing Guide* to help you decide if investing in your child's name is expected to adversely affect his or her ability to qualify for financial aid.

State Education Bonds

A few states sell bonds designed for college savings. These bonds normally pay a fixed interest rate that is exempt from federal and state taxes, even if you don't use the savings for education. The bonds may also provide financial incentives for your child to attend an in-state school.

Call your bank to see if your state offers these bonds. Ask about the interest rate. Keep in mind that a bond paying 4% tax-free is comparable to a taxable investment earning 6% (assuming a 28% federal tax and 5% state tax).[1] Each new bond issue might have different rules, so read the terms carefully.

☐ Where NOT to Save

Series EE U.S. Savings Bonds

Series EE Savings Bonds are government insured bonds that earn interest which is exempt from state and local taxes. And if you cash in bonds to pay college expenses, you might also qualify to avoid federal taxes if you meet certain conditions.

Do not put your savings in these bonds, because even with all the tax breaks your money can grow faster invested elsewhere. Furthermore, you can't be

[1] $\text{Taxable Return} = 6\% = \frac{4\%}{100\% - (28\% + 5\%)} \times 100\% = \frac{\text{Tax Free Return}}{100\% - \text{Tax Rate}} \times 100\%$

certain you'll qualify for the federal tax break—the most significant of the tax incentives.

Before you cash in any bonds, jot down each bond's issue date. Then phone the Federal Reserve at 800-553-2663 to learn when interest is posted for each bond. Cash in bonds immediately after the posting date, because you don't get interest for a partial period. **If you have MANY bonds to cash in**, you may need to spread your redemptions over several years. Bond interest counts as income on your tax return, so make sure you are not sending yourself into a higher tax bracket.

If you have some bonds you wish to keep for college, here's how to avoid the federal taxes.

- Bonds must show an issue date of 1990 or later.
- Bonds must be issued to someone age 24 or older.
- Bonds must be issued in a parent's name (not a child's name).
- Bonds must be redeemed in a year you pay qualified educational expenses for yourself, your spouse, or a child. Qualified expenses include tuition and fees, but not room and board or books.
- In the year you redeem bonds, your adjusted gross income must fall below a certain limit. Beyond this limit, the tax break phases out. So, consider the following.
  - —Between now and the time you redeem bonds, will your income rise faster than this limit? (The limit is indexed to inflation.)
  - —Will a spouse return to work sending you over the limit?
  - —Will the interest from the bonds you redeem to pay college expenses put your income over the limit?

  For the 1996 tax year, the tax break phases out for unmarried persons with income between $43,500 and $58,500, and for couples filing jointly with income between $65,250 and $95,250. Couples filing separate returns do not qualify for the tax break.

Plan to hold bonds for at least five years to get the long-term interest rate. Don't worry if bonds will reach maturity before college. You don't have to redeem them when they mature, and they pay interest for 30 years.

For more information about Series EE bonds, ask your bank for a brochure, or contact the Office of Public Affairs, U.S. Savings Bonds Division, Washington, DC 20226.

CollegeSure Certificates of Deposit

One bank offers a certificate of deposit called the *CollegeSure CD.* This CD is unique because the interest it pays is tied to the annual rise in college costs. This investment presents several drawbacks:

- Your money can grow faster invested elsewhere.
- You get no special tax breaks.
- There are substantial penalties for early withdrawal—10% of principal during the first three years, 5% thereafter until the year before maturity when the penalty drops to 1%.

If you want more information about this CD, phone the College Savings Bank at 800-888-2723.

Prepaid Tuition Programs

A few states guarantee to pay your child's tuition—whatever the future cost—in exchange for a set payment now. This savings approach may sound like a good idea, but it is not:

- Your money can grow faster invested elsewhere.
- Your payment(s) to the program do not avoid gift taxes (even if they fall under $10,000 per year—the usual gift tax exclusion).
- You do not have free and easy access to your money in the event of an emergency.
- You must pursue a refund if your child skips college, is not admitted, drops out, or attends a school that is not part of the program. Refund policies range from good (your money back with interest) to ghastly (no interest *and* a cancellation fee).
- During college, your child will pay income tax on your investment's earnings (calculated as the difference between the actual cost of school and the amount paid into the program).

If you want to learn more about the program offered in your state, contact a state university's financial aid office.

Annuities

Annuities are tax-deferred savings plans sold by insurance companies.

Do not use annuities to save for college. Annuities are retirement investments, as their rules reflect. For instance, if you withdraw money from an annuity before you turn 59½, you pay a 10% penalty to the federal government on the tax-deferred portion of your withdrawal. (Your state may also levy a penalty.)

If you currently use annuities to save for college, consider them as part of your retirement plan instead, and return to the worksheet on page 13 to recalculate your college savings needs. (Reduce the Value of current savings for each child by each child's share of the annuities.)

Cash-Value Life Insurance

Cash-value life insurance includes products such as *whole life*, *ordinary life*, *universal life*, *variable life*, *variable universal life*, *adjustable life*, *single-premium life*, and others similarly named. These products combine life insurance with a tax-deferred savings plan.

Do not use cash-value life insurance to save for college. These policies are poor investments.

If you currently use such insurance to save for college, consider these policies as part of your life insurance plan instead, and return to the worksheet on page 13 to recalculate your college savings needs. (Reduce the Value of current savings for each child by each child's share of the cash values.)

Emergency Savings

Emergency savings serve as a financial cushion when an unexpected event interrupts your income or increases your expenses, such as a lay-off, short-term disability, or major car repair. Without these savings, you must either go into debt or spend savings earmarked for another purpose. Neither alternative is good: you pay finance charges on debt, and you sacrifice your financial goals if you do not replenish your savings with interest.

☐ How Much Savings Do You Need?

You should have emergency savings equal to six months of your net income. To calculate these savings, divide your net annual income by 2 and enter the result below. Turn to page 50 for assistance in determining your net income.

Emergency Savings = ____________

If you cannot immediately set aside these savings, use payroll deduction or automatic withdrawal to accumulate them (see page 8).

Whenever you must spend this money, replace it as soon as possible.

☐ Where to Save

Keep roughly 20% of these savings in a money market mutual fund. This kind of fund pays more interest than a bank savings account and offers you a checkbook for immediate access to your money. Invest the remainder in a mutual fund that offers greater potential return. Refer to page 99 for more information about mutual funds.

LIFE INSURANCE

Sources of Protection 18
How Much Life Insurance Do You Need? 19
The Rule of Thumb 19
The Worksheet 19
Life Insurance For Children 19
Life Insurance During Retirement 20

If you have children, a spouse, or others who rely on your income, you may need life insurance to ensure that this income will continue upon your death.

☐ Sources of Protection

You have several potential sources of financial protection in the event of a death.

- **Privately-Paid Life Insurance** can replace all of your income. This is the most common form of life insurance.
- **Employer-Paid Life Insurance** often provides protection equal to one year's income. You may need more coverage than this, and if you leave your job, you might lose this coverage.
- **Risk Sharing Pools** are state-sponsored programs that make insurance available to high-risk individuals. If you cannot obtain coverage through other means, call your state insurance department and ask if a risk sharing pool operates in your state.
- **Your Spouse** may be able to replace some of your income by increasing his or her earnings after your death. This added income lowers your insurance needs.
- **Savings** provide economical protection if your insurance needs are small, or if you have substantial savings available.
- **Social Security Survivorship** can provide income to help raise your children. This benefit can also supplement your surviving spouse's income during retirement.
- **Workers' Compensation Survivorship** can provide generous benefits to your surviving family, but your death must be work-related. (Agricultural workers, domestic workers, and the self-employed are typically not covered.)
- **Veterans' Survivorship** can provide benefits to your surviving family, but your death must be related to your service in the military.

You need privately-paid life insurance when the other sources of protection do not provide adequate or assured coverage. The following discussion will help you determine *how much* life insurance you need.

How Much Life Insurance Do You Need?

Presented below are two methods for determining your life insurance needs—a rule of thumb and a comprehensive worksheet.

The Rule of Thumb

You should not use the rule of thumb to form your final estimate of life insurance needs, because it may leave you grossly under- or over-insured. Instead, you should take the time to complete the comprehensive worksheet (discussed below). Use the rule of thumb to quickly judge the adequacy of your current coverage. This assessment will help you determine if you should focus your current efforts on a different part of your financial plan.

The first step in using the rule of thumb is to determine if you need *any* life insurance at all. Typically, if no other person depends on your income, you do not need insurance. However, if someone *does* depend on your income, estimate your insurance needs by multiplying your gross annual income (determined on page 50) by the multiplier corresponding to your age from the table at the right. Do the same for your spouse using his or her gross annual income. You will notice that the multiplier decreases as you age to reflect your reduced need for insurance as you approach retirement.

RULE OF THUMB

Age	Multiplier
25 or younger	9
26 – 30	8
31 – 35	7
36 – 40	6
41 – 45	5
46 – 50	4
51 – 55	3
56 – 60	2
61 to retirement	1

The Worksheet

On page 59 you will find a worksheet to help you calculate your life insurance needs. The worksheet may be your most cumbersome planning task, so please don't get discouraged. When you finish the worksheet, turn to page 76 to learn about policy types and to shop for coverage.

Life Insurance For Children

Do not insure the lives of your children unless you depend on them for income. Even funeral and other final expenses are not worth covering. Use college savings or emergency savings to pay such expenses.

□ Life Insurance During Retirement

Your need for life insurance should end completely by retirement. Here's why. During your working years, life insurance protects income you might not live to earn. But during retirement, your savings provide income whether you live or not.

Short-Term Disability Insurance

Statistics show that a person is several times more likely to become disabled than to die before retirement. Also, a disability poses more severe financial consequences than a death due to the cost of caring for the disabled person. Do not neglect this vital part of your financial plan.

☐ Sources of Protection

You have several potential sources of income during a short-term disability (a disability lasting six months or less).

- **Sick Leave** through your employer provides 100% of your income, but this leave is unlikely to last for six months.
- **Employer-Paid Disability Insurance** can replace most of your income.
- **Privately-Paid Disability Insurance** can replace most of your income. However, it is expensive to include short-term protection in these policies.
- **Your Spouse** may be able to replace some of your income by increasing his or her earnings after your disability. However, if you and your spouse are disabled at the same time, this may not be possible.
- **Savings** can replace all of your income.
- **Workers' Compensation Disability** can replace much of your income, but your disability must be work-related. (Agricultural workers, domestic workers, and the self-employed are typically not covered.)
- **Veterans' Disability** can provide benefits, but your disability must be related to your service in the military.
- **California, Hawaii, New Jersey, New York, Rhode Island, and Puerto Rico** pay limited benefits for non-work-related disabilities. Contact your state government for more information.

☐ Savings Are Your Best Protection

To guarantee your income during a short-term disability, keep emergency savings equal to six months of your net income. Emergency savings are discussed on page 17.

LONG-TERM DISABILITY INSURANCE

How Much Protection Do You Need? 22
Sources of Protection 22
Employer-Paid Insurance 23
Privately-Paid Insurance 23
Savings 23
How Much Privately-Paid Insurance Do You Need? 24

Statistics show that a person is several times more likely to become disabled than to die before retirement. Also, a disability poses more severe financial consequences than a death due to the cost of caring for the disabled person. Do not neglect this vital part of your financial plan.

☐ How Much Protection Do You Need?

For a disability lasting six months or more, make sure that at least 80% of your net income (or about 60% of your gross income) is replaced until retirement. Although your income needs might actually increase after a disability, insurance companies will generally not insure you for more than 80% of your income because they want you to have a financial incentive to return to work.

☐ Sources of Protection

You have several potential sources of income during a long-term disability (a disability lasting more than six months).

- **Employer-Paid Disability Insurance** can replace most of your income. Although it might be expensive or impossible for you to replace this coverage if you leave your job, you may choose to rely on it anyway due to the high cost of private insurance.
- **Privately-Paid Disability Insurance** can replace most of your income. While it guarantees protection until retirement, policies often cost more than $1,000 per year.
- **Risk Sharing Pools** are state-sponsored programs that make insurance available to high-risk individuals. If you cannot obtain coverage through other means, call your state insurance department and ask if a risk sharing pool operates in your state.

- **Your Spouse** may be able to replace some of your income by increasing his or her earnings after your disability. However, if you and your spouse are disabled at the same time, this may not be possible.
- **Savings** provide economical protection if your insurance needs are small, or if you have substantial savings available.
- **Social Security Disability** can supplement your income beginning six months after you become disabled, but qualifying is difficult and depends on your disability[1] and work history.
- **Workers' Compensation Disability** can replace much of your income, but your disability must be work-related. (Agricultural workers, domestic workers, and the self-employed are typically not covered.)
- **Veterans' Disability** can provide benefits, but your disability must be related to your service in the military.

Employer-Paid Insurance

Compare the features of your employer plan to those described on pages 85 through 87. Also, find out if you can take the insurance with you if you leave your job. Your comfort level with these factors will help you decide whether or not to rely on this coverage.

If you become disabled, the amount of your benefits from an employer policy will depend on whether or not you paid income tax on your employer's premiums. If you *did* pay this tax, then your benefits are tax free. If you *did not* pay this tax, then your benefits are taxable as income. The worksheet beginning on page 25 will help you calculate your coverage needs.

Privately-Paid Insurance

Benefits from privately-paid insurance are tax free. Therefore, a policy that pays 60% of your gross income should provide sufficient coverage.

In most cases, private insurance will only allow you to protect earned income—income reported on a W-2. This means that you normally cannot buy insurance to protect the value of your services to the family, such as cleaning and child care. For these situations, personal savings is your only alternative.

Savings

Whether you have employer-paid insurance, privately-paid insurance, or both, it is a good idea to increase your coverage with personal savings. Savings provide guaranteed protection that may allow you to gradually reduce your need for expensive private insurance. Furthermore, if you never become disabled, you can retire early or with a larger income.

Retirement investments are the best places for these savings. They offer excellent tax breaks, and all of them (except a few employer plans) allow

[1] Social Security defines a disability as an injury or illness severe enough to keep you from substantial gainful activity for at least 12 months. The disability can be physical or mental, but it must be medically determinable.

you to withdraw your money without penalty in the event of a disability.[1] If it happens that your disability does not qualify to avoid the penalty, minimize the penalty by withdrawing money from your retirement savings in the following order: stock mutual funds held outside of a retirement account, cash-value life insurance, annuities, IRAs, and employer plans.

If you want to set aside savings for long-term disability protection, go back to your retirement calculations and investigate the additional savings needs for an early retirement. When you find a savings increase you believe you can afford, return to page 5 for investment advice. Be sure to keep a separate record of your disability savings so you don't accidentally spend your retirement savings during a disability.

☐ How Much Privately-Paid Insurance Do You Need?

Use the worksheet on the following page to estimate your need for privately-paid insurance. Note that the worksheet does not give you the option to rely on Social Security, Workers' Compensation, or Veterans' Disability benefits. You should not count on these programs because your disability might not qualify for their benefits. However, the existence of these programs can lower your insurance premiums. The shopping instructions (beginning on page 85) will tell you *how* and will help you shop for quality, low-cost disability insurance.

NOTE: If you or your spouse relies on alimony, child support, or other such income from a former partner, this income should be protected in case the former partner becomes disabled. Such protection may already be in place because it is often required under the terms of separation. However, if this protections is not in place, purchase disability insurance on your former partner equal to the annual income they provide.

---

[1] To avoid withdrawal penalties, your disability must satisfy the IRS's definition of disability (which is essentially the same as Social Security's definition)—an injury or illness severe enough to keep you from substantial gainful activity for at least 12 months.

LONG-TERM DISABILITY WORKSHEET

This worksheet helps you estimate *your* need (denoted *you*) and *your spouse's* need (denoted *sps*) for privately-paid disability insurance. As you complete the worksheet, do not attempt to adjust your entries for cost-of-living increases or inflation. The worksheet already accounts for these.[1]

A Gross Income — **A** __________

On line **A**, enter your Gross Annual Income (from the Total column on page 50).

B Income Goal — **B** __________ (**A** x 0.6)

Experts suggest that you should protect at least 60% of your gross income. To calculate this income goal, multiply your gross income **A** by 0.6. Enter the result on line **B**.

EMPLOYER-PAID INSURANCE

C Gross Income Expected — **C***you* __________ **C***sps* __________

In blank **C***you*, enter the annual disability income *you* expect from employer-paid insurance. Ask your benefits coordinator for this number. **Do the same for your spouse.** In blank **C***sps*, enter the annual disability income *your spouse* expects from employer-paid insurance.

D Net Income Expected — **D***you* __________ (**C***you* or (**C***you* x 0.7)) **D***sps* __________ (**C***sps* or (**C***sps* x 0.7))

If you pay tax on your employer's disability premiums, copy your income from **C***you* into blank **D***you*. If you don't pay tax on employer premiums, multiply **C***you* by 0.7 to approximate your benefit after taxes, and enter the result in blank **D***you*. **Do the same for your spouse.** If your spouse pays taxes on employer premiums, copy the income from **C***sps* into blank **D***sps*. Otherwise, multiply **C***sps* by 0.7 to approximate the benefit after taxes, and enter the result in blank **D***sps*.

SAVINGS

E Value of Savings Set Aside — **E***you* __________ **E***sps* __________

In blank **E***you*, enter the total savings set aside for *your* long-term disability protection. In blank **E***sps*, enter the amount of savings set aside for *your spouse*.

F Number of Years Until Retirement — **F***you* __________ **F***sps* __________

In blank **F***you*, enter the number of years between now and the time *you* will retire. In blank **F***sps*, enter the number of years between now and the time *your spouse* will retire.

G Income Expected — **G***you* __________ (**E***you* ÷ **F***you*) **G***sps* __________ (**E***sps* ÷ **F***sps*)

Divide your savings **E** by the number of years until you retire **F** to estimate the annual income your savings can provide.

---

[1] The worksheet assumes your income goal and savings grow at the rate of inflation. These assumptions simplify the worksheet significantly. The first assumption allows you to enter all future incomes in today's dollars. The second allows you to ignore the growth rate of your savings. This second assumption is probably conservative, because your long-term savings are likely to grow faster than inflation.

LONG-TERM DISABILITY WORKSHEET

... continued

SPOUSE

H Income Expected H_{you} ___________ H_{sps} ___________

In blank H_{you}, enter the annual net income (income after taxes) your spouse expects to earn if *you* become disabled. If your spouse expects to earn the Net Annual Income shown under Spouse on page 50, simply copy this value into blank H_{you}. **Do the same for your spouse.** In blank H_{sps}, enter the annual net income *you* expect to earn if *your spouse* becomes disabled. If you expect to earn the Net Annual Income shown under You on page 50, simply copy this value into blank H_{sps}.

RESULT

I Amount of Privately-Paid Disability Insurance Needed

Determine your needs for privately-paid insurance by subtracting from your income goal **B** the incomes expected from your employer **D**, savings **G**, and spouse **H**. Turn to page 85 to shop for this coverage or to cancel unneeded policies.

I_{you} ___________ ($B - D_{you} - G_{you} - H_{you}$)

I_{sps} ___________ ($B - D_{sps} - G_{sps} - H_{sps}$)

HEALTH INSURANCE

Without health insurance, financial ruin can come quickly. Make sure every member of your family is insured against major health care costs.

☐ How Much Protection Do You Need?

Your family limit of protection should be at least one million dollars.

☐ Sources of Protection

You have several potential sources for health care protection:

- **Group Health Insurance** through your employer or elsewhere can provide comprehensive medical protection to you and your family. If you leave your job (or are no longer a member of the group) the insurer might be required to offer you a conversion policy, even if you or a family member are uninsurable. Group insurance is the most economical form of coverage.
- **Private Health Insurance** is expensive, but may be your only choice for protecting you and your family. If you need this coverage, turn to page 90 for more information.
- **Risk Sharing Pools** are state-sponsored programs that make insurance available to high-risk individuals. If you cannot obtain coverage through group or private insurance, call your state insurance department and ask if a risk sharing pool operates in your state.
- **Workers' Compensation Health** provides comprehensive medical benefits, but only if your illness or injuries are work-related. (Agricultural workers, domestic workers, and the self-employed are typically not covered.)
- **Veterans' Health** can provide benefits, but your medical needs must be related to your service in the military.
- **Medicare** provides medical benefits to people over 65 and to the disabled.
- **Medicaid** provides medical benefits to the poor.

☐ Health Plan Options to Avoid

Your group or private plan may allow you to pay extra for dental, maternity, prescription drug, and supplemental accident benefits. These coverages are typically not a good value unless your employer pays a significant portion of the premiums.

- For **Dental**, **Maternity**, and **Prescription Drug** coverages, judge value for yourself. For each coverage, compare high and low estimates of your actual medical costs to the total of your premiums, deductibles, and expenses that exceed the limits of coverage. You may find it cheaper to pay these costs yourself. Note that your basic health plan may already cover dental surgery and pregnancy complications. Also, your newborn child is automatically covered as long as you properly notify your insurance company of the upcoming birth.

- **Supplemental Accident** coverage pays your deductible only when medical costs result from an accident. If you truly need a lower deductible, then you need it to apply in all cases, not just for accidents.

LIABILITY INSURANCE

Liability insurance protects your wealth and income in the event you cause harm to others or their property. Your home and auto insurance policies include this coverage up to the limits you selected. But how did you select these limits? If you are like most people, you relied on the recommendations of the person selling you the coverage—recommendations often based on little or no analysis of your actual needs. This chapter helps you set reasonable limits for your home and auto liability protection. It also suggests when you should seek the added protection of umbrella liability insurance.

☐ How Much Protection Do You Need?

One rule of thumb suggests that you should have coverage equal to your net worth plus twice your income. Another rule suggests protection equal to twice your net worth. Use the worksheet below to estimate the protection suggested by each of these methods. Set your liability limits based on the method that produces the largest value.

Although these rules of thumb serve as useful guides, there is no guarantee that any amount of protection you carry will be enough. For instance, if the damages you cause to someone are difficult to quantify, such as pain and suffering, you can easily be sued beyond the limits of your liability insurance. It is impractical, if not impossible, to protect yourself against such accidents. Therefore, you should plan to protect yourself to reasonable limits.

If the suggested limit for your liability protection exceeds $300,000, or if you simply feel more comfortable having greater coverage, consider supplementing your home and auto liability insurance with umbrella liability (described on the next page).

LIABILITY WORKSHEET

	Method One	Method Two
Gross Annual Income *(from the Total column on page 50)*	2 x ________	
Net Worth *(from page 51)* If your estimated net worth is negative, write zeros in the blanks.	+ ________	2 x ________
Total Calculate the total for each method.	= ________	= ________

Suggested Limit for Liability Protection ________
Round the larger total up to the nearest $50,000 or $100,000, and write the result in the blank.

☐ Umbrella Liability Insurance

Umbrella liability is an inexpensive way to extend the liability limits of your home and auto policies by a million dollars or more, while providing you with greater protection including libel, slander, defamation of character, invasion of privacy, false arrest, and wrongful eviction. (Work-related liability is normally not covered.)

Umbrella liability costs between $100 and $200 per year. You usually purchase such a policy in conjunction with your home and auto insurance, so all three policies come from the same company.

$300,000 is chosen as the threshold for considering umbrella liability insurance because it is a standard liability limit for many home and auto policies. Beyond $300,000, home and auto limits tend to be farther apart. For instance, your next choice might be $500,000. Instead of raising the limits for both your home and auto above $300,000, consider purchasing umbrella liability insurance. The instructions beginning on page 91 will help you shop for umbrella liability while you shop for home and auto insurance.

HOME INSURANCE

Whether you own or rent, home insurance provides valuable financial protection. It helps you replace damaged or stolen property, and it compensates others when you injure them or their property.

☐ How Much Protection Do You Need?

Your home insurance should include the coverages described in the table below. The terms shown in bold are explained on the following pages, along with some other coverage options. The instructions beginning on page 91 will help you shop for quality, low-cost home insurance.

HOME INSURANCE
Dwelling *If you RENT . . .* You do not need dwelling coverage because you do not own your building. *If you OWN A CONDOMINIUM . . .* Your association may insure most of your dwelling. Read the association's policy. If you need some dwelling coverage, insure to 100% of **replacement cost** with **inflation protection** for no fewer than the standard set of 17 perils.[1] *If you OWN A HOUSE OR MANUFACTURED HOME . . .* Insure your home to 100% of the structure's **replacement cost** with **inflation protection** for no fewer than the standard set of 17 perils.[1] *If you OWN AN OLDER HOME . . .* An older home containing fine materials and craftsmanship might cost far more to rebuild than its market value. In this case, the most practical choice may be to insure your home to 100% of its **actual cash value** with **inflation protection** for the standard set of 11 perils.[1] (These policies do not cover the last 6 perils.)
Personal Property Your personal possessions should be insured to their **replacement cost** for no fewer than the standard set of 17 perils.[1]
Deductible You should select a deductible of $500 or more to reduce your premiums.
Liability Use the Suggested Limit for Liability Protection from the worksheet on page 29. ($1,000 of **medical payments to others** is usually included automatically.)

[1] The first 11 perils include fire & lightning, windstorm & hail, explosion, riots, aircraft, vehicles, smoke, vandalism, theft, glass breakage, and volcanic eruption. The remaining 6 include falling objects, weight of ice, snow & sleet, and damage to plumbing, heating, air conditioning, electrical wiring & appliances due to ice, water, steam & electrical current.

Dwelling

Your dwelling includes the building you live in and other structures nearby, such as a detached garage or storage shed. Your coverage should include rebuilding costs only. It should not include the value of your land, because land holds its value with or without the buildings.

Inflation Protection

This term applies to dwelling coverage. Inflation protection means that your insurance company adjusts your coverage and premium regularly to reflect increasing construction costs in your area.

Personal Property

Personal property refers to your household possessions. Most policies automatically insure your personal property up to one-half the value of your dwelling coverage. You can purchase additional coverage if you need it.

Replacement Cost *vs.* Actual Cash Value

These terms apply to your dwelling and personal property coverages. A replacement cost policy pays the amount needed to rebuild your home or to replace personal property. An actual cash value policy pays far less. It pays the replacement cost minus depreciation.

Deductible

The deductible is the part of a claim that you pay. Every claim you file, regardless of its size, costs the insurance company several hundred dollars to process. If you file small claims because you have a low deductible, your premiums must include these large administrative costs *and* the added coverage. Consequently, you can reduce your premiums 10% to 20% by increasing your deductible to $500 or $1,000. Use your emergency savings (discussed on page 17) to cover these higher deductibles.

Liability

Liability insurance covers bodily injury and property damage that you, a family member, or a pet cause to someone else. Purchase no less than the protection you calculated on page 29. Home insurance policies offer a limited selection of coverage levels, usually $100,000, $200,000, and $300,000. If you need more than $300,000 of protection, consider supplementing this coverage with umbrella liability insurance (see page 30).

Medical Payments to Others

This coverage pays medical and funeral expenses to someone who is injured or killed in an accident (other than an auto accident) that involves you, a family member, or a pet, even if you are not at fault. This coverage is unnecessary. If you *are* responsible for an accident, your liability coverage protects you. If you *are not* responsible for an accident, you have no financial liability. Take the minimum coverage allowed, usually $1,000 per person.

Standard Exclusions

Standard home policies do not cover losses due to wars, nuclear hazards, earthquakes, floods, laws & ordinances, animals, wear & tear, neglect, and intentional damage.

You can, however, buy coverage for some of these exclusions.

- **Earthquake Insurance** is normally available as a rider to your policy.
- **Flood Insurance** is often not available with your home policy. If you feel you need this coverage, call the National Flood Insurance Program at 800-638-6620.
- **Laws & Ordinances** is usually offered as a rider to your policy. Few people need it. It compensates you in the event that reconstruction of your home is more expensive or prohibited due to changes in zoning or building codes. This coverage is most common for properties located on shorelines and floodplains.

AUTO INSURANCE

Auto insurance helps pay the bills when your car is involved in an accident. Most states require minimum levels of coverage.

☐ How Much Protection Do You Need?

The passages following the table explain your coverage needs. Record these needs in the table below. The instructions beginning on page 91 will help you shop for quality, low-cost auto insurance.

AUTO INSURANCE

Liability*

Bodily Injury (BI)	________ per person		________ per accident *(set by insurer)*	
Property Damage (PD)			________ per accident	
	Auto 1	**Auto 2**	**Auto 3**	**Auto 4**
Collision & Comprehensive	YES NO	YES NO	YES NO	YES NO
Deductible	____ *($500 or more)*	____ *($500 or more)*	____ *($500 or more)*	____ *($500 or more)*

UNinsured Motorist*

Bodily Injury (BI)	________ per person *(minimum)*	________ per accident *(minimum)*
Property Damage (PD)		________ per accident *(minimum)*

Personal Injury Protection (PIP)* ________ *(minimum)* Deductible ________ *(maximum)*

* Your state might require certain levels of liability, uninsured motorist, and personal injury protection. Call your state insurance department for these limits. If your state's phone number is shown in bold, ask for an auto insurance shopping guide as well.

AL	**334-269-3550**	IA	515-281-5705	MO	**800-726-7390**	PR	809-722-8686
AK	**907-269-7900**	ID	800-721-3272	MT	**800-332-6148**	RI	**401-277-2223**
AZ	**602-912-8444**	IL	217-782-4515	NE	**402-471-2201**	SC	**800-768-3467**
AR	800-852-5494	IN	800-622-4461	NV	**800-992-0900**	SD	605-773-3563
CA	**800-927-4357**	KS	800-432-2484	NH	800-852-3416	TN	800-342-4029
CO	**303-894-7499**	KY	**502-564-3630**	NJ	**800-446-7467**	TX	**800-252-3439**
CT	**203-297-3867**	LA	**800-259-5300**	NM	800-947-4722	UT	**800-439-3805**
DE	**800-282-8611**	MA	**617-521-7777**	NY	**800-342-3736**	VT	**802-828-3301**
DC	202-727-8000	MD	**800-492-6116**	NC	800-662-7777	VI	809-774-2991
FL	**904-922-3132**	ME	**207-624-8475**	ND	**800-247-0560**	VA	**800-552-7945**
GA	404-656-2070	MI	**517-373-9273**	OH	**800-686-1526**	WA	**800-562-6900**
GU	671-477-1040	MN	**800-657-3602**	OK	800-522-0071	WV	**800-642-9004**
HI	**808-587-1234**	MS	800-562-2957	OR	**503-378-4484**	WI	**800-236-8517**
				PA	**717-787-2317**	WY	**800-438-5768**

Bodily Injury Liability

When the driver of your car causes an accident, bodily injury liability covers the injuries of everyone involved in the accident except the driver of your car, up to the limits of the policy. These limits typically define a *per person* maximum as well as a *per accident* maximum. Purchase *per person* coverage of at least the limit of protection you calculated on page 29. Normally, the *per accident* coverage is set by the insurer at two or three times the *per person* coverage. These coverages are sold in round numbers that vary by insurer. If you need more than $300,000 of protection, consider supplementing this coverage with umbrella liability insurance (see page 30).

If the driver of your car causes the accident, he or she is not covered by this insurance. This is another reason it is essential for everyone to have adequate health, disability, and life insurance protection.

Property Damage Liability

When the driver of your car causes damage to someone else's car or other property, property damage liability covers these costs up to the limits of the policy. Purchase at least the limit of protection you calculated on page 29. Again, if you need more than $300,000 of protection, consider supplementing this coverage with umbrella liability (see page 30).

Some Policies Combine Bodily Injury and Property Damage Liability

Some insurance companies offer single-limit liability protection instead of the split-limits just discussed. A single-limit policy does not divide your coverage into categories. With this type of policy, purchase at least the limit of protection you calculated on page 29. If you need more than $300,000 of protection, consider supplementing this coverage with umbrella liability (see page 30).

Collision and Comprehensive

Collision and comprehensive insurance provides coverage for most types of damage to your auto, regardless of who is at fault. Collision pays for damages caused by an accident, while comprehensive (sometimes called *other than collision*) pays for damages from most other causes, such as falling objects, flooding, or theft. You should carry these coverages for each auto having a book value of $2,000 or more. Find a current Red Book or Blue Book at the reference desk of your library to learn the book values of your cars.

This $2,000 threshold is simply a rule of thumb. You should select a value that makes you comfortable. But remember, at some point you are better off dropping your collision and comprehensive insurance and bearing the risks yourself. Here is an example to illustrate why.

> Consider two Chevy Cavaliers, nearly identical except that one is six years older than the other. The newer car is worth $7,900 and costs $140 per year to insure for collision and comprehensive with a $500 deductible, while the older car is worth $2,700 and costs $100 to insure with the same deductible. If the newer Cavalier is totalled in an

accident (meaning the cost of repair exceeds the car's book value), the owner collects the value of the car minus the deductible, or $7,400. If the older Cavalier is totalled, the owner collects $2,200. So, in one case the owner pays $140 for $7,400 of protection, and in the other case the owner pays $100 for $2,200 of protection. As you can see, your car's value will decline more swiftly than the insurance premiums.

To keep your premiums low, choose a high deductible. Raising a $100 deductible to $500 or $1,000 can lower premiums by 35% or 60%. (A high deductible costs less because you make fewer claims, and every claim, large or small, costs the insurance company several hundred dollars in administrative expenses that they must recoup through premiums.) Use your emergency savings (discussed on page 17) to cover this higher deductible.

UNinsured and UNDERinsured Motorist

If you, your passengers, or your property are hurt by someone driving **without** insurance, UNinsured motorist pays your bills up to the limits of your policy. If the at-fault driver *is* insured, but with coverage that is insufficient to pay your claims, UNDERinsured motorist pays the difference. Half of the states require a minimum level of UNinsured motorist. None require UNDERinsured motorist.

You should not need these coverages because they duplicate the health, disability, and life insurance protection you and your passengers should already have. Also, the damage to your car is covered by your collision insurance (if you have it). Take the minimum coverage allowed by your state.

Personal Injury Protection (PIP)

If you, your passengers, or your property are damaged in an auto accident, personal injury protection pays benefits no matter who is at fault. This coverage duplicates the health, disability, life, and collision insurance you and your passengers should already have. Take the minimum coverage and the highest deductible allowed by your state.

Road Service and Rental Reimbursement

If your car breaks down, road service pays towing and labor expenses (but not parts) up to a limit, usually between $25 and $75. Rental reimbursement pays between $10 and $15 per day toward a rental car while your car is in the shop. These coverages are not a good value. It is more economical to use emergency savings to cover these expenses.

Medical Payments, Dismemberment, Loss of Sight, Disability, & Death

Do not purchase these coverages because they duplicate protection you and your passengers should already have through health, disability, and life insurance. Also, these coverages only apply to automobile-related incidents. If you need these protections, you need them all the time.

When Renting a Car

In most cases, you should refuse the insurance offered when you rent a car. Your personal auto policy probably covers you. Call your insurance company to make sure (especially if you'll be driving outside the U.S.). If you rent with a credit card, your card may cover you also. Check with your credit card company for details. There are, however, a few situations where you should buy coverage from the rental car company.

- A **damage waiver** provides collision and comprehensive coverage on your rental car. Purchase this waiver if neither your personal auto policy nor your credit card provide this protection when you rent.
- A **liability insurance supplement** adds liability coverage to the amount already carried by the rental car company. Do not purchase this supplement if:
  (1) you have umbrella liability insurance,
  (2) your personal auto policy applies when you rent a car, or
  (3) your credit card provides adequate liability coverage.

  If you need liability protection, find out the rental company's liability coverage in the state where you rent the car. If the company's coverage plus your credit card's coverage fall short of your needs, purchase the liability insurance supplement.

When Renting a Truck or Trailer

Most personal auto policies **do not** cover these types of rentals. Read your policy or call your insurer. You will probably need to buy the insurance offered by the rental company.

ESTATE PLANNING FOR SEVERE DISABILITY

If poor health makes you unable to make important decisions, you will want your wishes to be known, and you will want a loved one to have the legal right to honor them. Therefore, each adult in your family should prepare the following documents. Without them, the legal system will make decisions for you at great expense to your family.

- A **Living Will** conveys your wishes regarding life-sustaining medical procedures.
- A **Power of Attorney for Health Care** authorizes the person you choose to make health care decisions for you.
- A **Power of Attorney for Financial Matters** (often abbreviated *Power of Attorney*) authorizes the person you choose to make financial decisions for you.[1]

If you have access to a personal computer, you can prepare these documents quickly and easily using special software. Ordering instructions appear on page 41.

If you do not have access to a personal computer, phone your state health department, your state medical society, your health care provider, or your local library to see if they offer blank versions of these documents. Otherwise, you can find them at an office supply store.

For further reading, find a self-help law book such as Denis Clifford's *The Power of Attorney Book.*

---

[1] This document is unnecessary if all of your property is in a living trust.

ESTATE PLANNING FOR DEATH

Upon your death, you want your heirs cared for and your property distributed according to your instructions, in a timely fashion, with little administrative expense, and with minimal taxation. To achieve these goals, you must prepare legal documents and carefully arrange your property (names on accounts, names on titles, beneficiary designations, etc.). The complexity of your personal situation should dictate the documents you need and the subsequent arrangement of your property. The following passages will help you assess your situation.

Wills

In all cases, you should have a will. (You and your spouse should have separate wills.) A will is essential no matter how simple or complex your estate. For a simple estate, a will is the sole means for communicating wishes, including the choice of a guardian for children and the distribution of property. For a complicated estate, a will might simply govern the small amount property that is not controlled by other legal documents.

Trusts Established At Death

A trust is a legal entity (similar to a person) that holds title to property. It is governed by a document that tells the appointed trustee how to manage and dispense the property. Use the following guidelines to help you decide if your will should establish a trust upon your death.

- **The surviving spouse (or other heir) is an unskilled money manager.**
  A trust allows you to choose a trusted professional, friend, or family member to manage your estate. Use a trust when your life insurance benefits must supply years of income to survivors, and you question their ability to handle this money without guidance. Also, use a trust when you want to control the distribution of wealth to a child or young adult.
- **You want to prevent a beneficiary's spouse or creditors from reaching inherited property.**
  A trust allows you to shield your property.
- **You are married and your estate is worth more than $600,000, but less than $1,200,000.**
  A trust allows you to avoid estate taxes in this case. If you are married, use the following worksheet to estimate the value of your estate.

YOUR ESTATE — MARRIED		
Net Worth	(from page 51)	________
Total Employer-Paid Life Insurance	(**FF***you* + **FF***sps* from page 71)	________
Total Privately-Paid Life Insurance	(**HH***you* + **HH***sps* from page 71)	________
Value of Your Estate	(add the numbers listed above)	________

Trusts Established Before Death

You may want to place some (or all) of your property in a trust *now* instead of waiting until your death. Consider this option in the following situations.

- **The surviving spouse (or other heir) is an unskilled money manager.**
  (See the explanation on the previous page.)
- **You want to prevent a beneficiary's spouse or creditors from reaching inherited property.**
  A trust allows you to shield your property.
- **Your heirs need immediate access to your property (such as to operate a family business).**
  A trust allows you to avoid probate's temporary hold on your assets. (Probate is the court procedure for settling your estate.)
- **You own real estate in more than one state (or you feel probate is too expensive in your state).**
  A trust allows you to avoid the cost and hassle of filing probate documents in each jurisdiction in which you own property. Call the local probate court for each of your properties to determine the potential filing fees. (Some courts charge a flat fee. Some take a percentage of the property probated. And some take a percentage of your total estate regardless of the amount probated.)
- **You want privacy regarding the distribution of your property.**
  A trust allows you to avoid probate's reporting requirements. (When you use a will as the only means to distribute property, public notices are placed in newspapers, and copies of your will are sent to relatives even if they will not inherit property.)
- **You are married and your estate is worth more than $1,200,000.**
  For large estates, trusts established prior to death offer greater potential tax savings than trusts created by a will.[1]
- **You are single and your estate is worth more than $600,000.**
  Trusts established prior to death allow you to minimize estate taxes. If you are single, use the following worksheet to estimate the value of your estate.[1]

---

[1] This statement refers to the establishment of **irrevocable trusts**, such as life insurance trusts, crummy trusts, and split-interest trusts. It does not refer to the establishment of **revocable trusts** (living trusts) which offer no more tax savings than trusts created by wills.

YOUR ESTATE — SINGLE		
Net Worth	(from page 51)	____________
Employer-Paid Life Insurance	(S from page 61)	____________
Privately-Paid Life Insurance	(U from page 61)	____________
Value of Your Estate	(add the numbers listed above)	____________

The cost of your estate plan will increase as you move from a simple will—$100 or more—to the more complicated techniques involving trusts—$1,000 or more. Minimize this cost through a little preparation. Before you hire an attorney, attempt to prepare your own documents using a do-it-yourself book or software package. The information you gather and the knowledge you gain from this exercise will save you money by speeding communication with your attorney.

Here are some good sources of do-it-yourself information.

- *Nolo's Simple Will Book* and *Make Your Own Living Trust*—both by Denis Clifford—are excellent books. (Be sure to find a current edition of any book you choose.)
- If you have access to a personal computer, special software makes it faster and easier to draft your documents (including powers of attorney, living wills, and many more). One of the best products is *Quicken Family Lawyer* for Windows, DOS, or Macintosh. The cost is roughly $35 after postage and handling. To obtain this software, phone 800-811-0458. Ask the representative to review the computer requirements with you.

PUTTING IT ALL TOGETHER IN A BUDGET

So far, your efforts have focused on individual planning topics. It is now time to put all of the pieces together and see if you have a workable plan.

The following table helps you construct a simple budget. On your first pass through the table, do your best to estimate your income and expenses. When you are finished, compare the totals. If your expenses exceed your income, you will need to make a second pass through the table and either cut your expenses or increase your income.

HOUSEHOLD BUDGET	
INCOME	
Earned Income Enter the net income you expect this year from employment. This income equals your take-home pay plus any amounts voluntarily deducted from your paycheck, such as retirement contributions, insurance premiums, and prepaid dental or child care.	________
Investment Income Enter the spendable income you expect this year from savings and other investments. (**Do not include** income earned on retirement savings, college savings, or other savings where the income is reinvested.)	________
Other Income Enter the income you expect this year from other sources, such as alimony, child support, trusts, Workers' Compensation, and Social Security.	________
Total Income Add the incomes listed above to determine your total available income for this year.	________
EXPENSES	
Retirement Savings Contributions Add the values from lines **C**, **E**, **F**, **G**, **H**, and **I** from the worksheet beginning on page 7. Enter the total here.	________
College Savings Contributions Add the Amount to save this year values from the worksheet on page 13. Enter the total here.	________
Emergency Savings Contributions Enter zero if you have adequate emergency savings (see page 17). Otherwise, enter the amount you will contribute this year to build these savings.	________

HOUSEHOLD BUDGET

. . . continued

Life Insurance Premiums __________
Enter the total amount you will pay for life insurance this year.

Disability Insurance Premiums __________
Enter the total amount you will pay for disability insurance this year.

Health Insurance Premiums __________
Enter the total amount you will pay for health insurance this year.

Liability, Home, & Auto Insurance Premiums __________
Enter the total amount you will pay for these insurances this year.

Alimony / Child Support __________
Enter the total amount you will pay this year in alimony and/or child support.

Taxes Not Withheld By Employer __________
If you will make quarterly estimated tax payments this year, enter the total of these payments.

Housing __________
Enter your total expected housing expense for this year, including rent or mortgage payments, property taxes, utilities, and upkeep.

Food __________
Enter your total expected food expense for this year.

Auto __________
Enter your total expected auto expense for this year. Include gas, maintenance, repairs, loan payments, and contributions to savings if you plan to pay cash for your next car. **Do not include** auto insurance premiums.

School / Child Care __________
Enter your total expected school and child care expenses for this year.

Medical / Dental __________
Enter your total expected medical expenses for this year. **Do not include** health or dental insurance premiums.

Clothing __________
Enter your total expected clothing expenses for this year.

Entertainment / Recreation __________
Enter your total expected leisure expenses for this year.

Gifts / Charitable Donations __________
Enter your total expected outlay for gifts and charitable contributions.

Other __________
Enter the total of all other expenses for this year.

Total Expenses __________
Add the expenses listed above to determine your total annual expenses.

From the table, compare your Total Income to your Total Expenses. If you have extra income, you have the luxury of pursuing more ambitious goals and/or improving your current standard of living. However, if you have an income shortage, you have two choices—raise your income or lower your expenses. To help you assess your expenses, the following table provides some general guidelines.

EXPENSE GUIDELINES	
Expense Category	**Suggested Maximum Percentage of Income**
Housing	35%
Food	15%
Auto	15%
School / Child Care	10%
Medical / Dental	5%
Clothing	5%
Entertainment / Recreation	5%
Gifts / Charitable Donations	10%
Other	10%

Your budgeting choices are not simple. They require trade-offs between your current living standard, your future living standard, and the cost to protect both of these from unpredictable events.

When To Update Your Financial Plan

It is important to update parts of your plan periodically and when significant events change your life. The following instructions will help you perform these updates efficiently.

Every Year . . .

Adjust your retirement and college savings contributions each year for inflation (cost-of-living increases). The worksheets on pages 7 and 13 include instructions for making these adjustments.

Revise your budget on page 42.

Every Few Years . . .

To make sure your college savings are on track, use the worksheet on page 13 to recalculate your savings needs. **Do not** use the same college costs you used previously. Instead, find more current numbers. If you want average costs, your mutual fund company can probably provide these. For current information about a particular school, call the school, or ask your librarian to help you find a recent college guidebook (such as *The College Handbook* by the College Entrance Examination Board).

As your income and net worth increase, you might need to increase your limits of liability protection. Use the information on page 29 to re-evaluate your liability insurance needs. Then review the home and auto liability information beginning on pages 31 and 34.

As you accumulate possessions, you might need to increase the property protection on your home insurance. The table on page 92 will help you inventory your possessions.

As your automobiles age, you may want to eliminate comprehensive and collision coverages. Review the discussion on page 35.

Every Five or Ten Years . . .

Ideally, you should completely re-evaluate your plan every five years. But don't wait more than ten years. If possible, begin your update six months before the renewal dates of your life and disability insurance policies so you have time to shop for new lower-priced policies. Also, don't forget to review your estate plan.

If Your Marital Status Changes . . .

You should completely re-evaluate your plan if you marry, divorce, or become widowed.

If You Expect a Child . . .

A new child will impact several parts of your financial plan. Review your college savings and life insurance needs, notify your health insurer of the coming child, and update your estate plan.

If Your Employer Benefits Change Significantly . . .

Employer benefits can include retirement savings, life insurance, disability insurance, and health insurance. Review the part of your plan affected by the change in benefits.

If Your Income Changes Unexpectedly . . .

You should completely re-evaluate your plan if your income changes significantly.

If You Change to a More or Less Hazardous Occupation . . .

The risk level of your occupation might impact your life, disability, and health insurance coverages.

- **If you change to a MORE hazardous occupation**, your premiums might increase. Read each policy carefully to see if your coverage depends on your occupation. If it does, notify the insurer of your job change and pay the higher premium. If a premium seems to jump unreasonably, shop for a new policy.
- **If you change to a LESS hazardous occupation**, contact your insurers and ask for lower premiums. If they refuse, shop for new policies to see if you can do better.

If You Move to a New State . . .

Your estate plan might not comply with the laws of your new state. Hire a competent estate planning attorney in the new state to review your documents.

If You Make a Major Home Improvement . . .

Be sure to notify your home insurer.

If You Buy a Car . . .

Be sure to notify your auto insurer.

WHERE TO GET HELP

If you need more detailed information, you can find it in consumer magazines, financial magazines, and books at your local library. Your mutual fund company is another good source for information.

If you decide to hire a financial planner, note the three types of planner.

- **Fee-Only Planners** charge a flat fee or an hourly rate for their services, but do not receive commissions from the insurance and investment products you buy. These planners do your calculations, research, and shopping. This arrangement offers the best chance that your interests will be served at the lowest possible cost.
- **Fee-Based Planners** charge a flat fee to do your calculations, and then also receive commissions from the insurance and investment products you buy. This arrangement may serve your interests, but probably not at the lowest possible cost, because these planners usually sell products for only a few companies, and sometimes only one. Furthermore, they have a financial incentive to sell you products you don't need and products that pay them higher commissions.
- **Commission-Only Planners** charge nothing for their advice, but rely solely on commissions from the insurance and investment products you buy. This arrangement may serve your interests, but probably not at the lowest possible cost, because these planners usually sell products for only a few companies, and sometimes only one. Furthermore, they have a financial incentive to sell you products you don't need and products that pay them higher commissions.

The best way to find a fee-only financial planner is through a personal recommendation. Whether or not you have a personal reference, you should phone the National Association of Personal Financial Advisors (NAPFA) at 800-366-2732 for a free interview form to help you select a planner. NAPFA will also provide you with names of Certified Financial Planners (CFPs) in your area. However, many excellent fee-only planners are not listed with this organization. When you call NAPFA, ask that your name remain confidential, otherwise you will be solicited by local agents.

To include fee-based and commission-only planners in your search, phone the Institute of Certified Financial Planners at 800-282-7526 for a similar list. Again, ask that your name remain confidential.

PART TWO

IMPLEMENT YOUR PLAN

YOUR INCOME

Much of financial planning deals with ensuring an adequate standard of living throughout your life. *Income* offers a convenient way to measure standard of living. This chapter helps you estimate your income for planning retirement savings, emergency savings, life insurance, disability insurance, and liability insurance.

Recording your income into the table below may be as simple as copying some numbers from your paystub. However, because the values you provide will be used to set important financial goals, make sure they accurately reflect the standard of living you expect for most of your working years. If, for instance, you or your spouse are temporarily out of the work force, then your current income *does not* accurately reflect your standard of living until retirement. In this case, you should provide incomes that assume you and your spouse are both working.

Please record both your gross income (earnings before taxes) and your net income (earnings after taxes) in the table below. Round these values to the nearest thousand dollars. For the purposes of this book, **do not include** earnings from savings and investments, and **do not include** income from a former partner, such as alimony, child support, Social Security Survivorship benefits, or life insurance benefits.

- If you know what your **gross income** will be for this year, record it in the table below. Otherwise, find your gross income on your final paystub from last year. (Gross income is expressed as total year-to-date earnings—often abbreviated YTD).
- Your **net income** equals your gross income minus federal, state, local, and FICA taxes. For a rough estimate, multiply your gross income by 0.7. (Your net income might not equal your take-home pay due to additional deductions such as retirement contributions or insurance premiums.)

INCOME					
	You		**Spouse**		**Total**
Gross Annual Income	________	+	________	=	________
Net Annual Income	________	+	________	=	________

YOUR NET WORTH

Your financial plan should protect your net worth. Your net worth is the value of what you *own* minus what you *owe*. Use the following table to help you estimate your net worth. Be sure to over-estimate rather than under-estimate, and do not try to be more accurate than the nearest $10,000.

NET WORTH

Total Value of Your Possessions $

- the current market value of your home and other real estate
- the current market value of your vehicles
- the current market value of your household belongings
  Imagine auctioning off all of your personal possessions. Roughly how much money would you collect?
- the current market value of your savings and investments
  Add the account balances or market values for your checking, savings, CDs, mutual funds, stocks, bonds, pensions (current lump-sum benefits) and other employer retirement plans, IRAs, and annuities. For your cash-value life insurance policies, add the cash values.

Total Value of Your Debts $

- the remaining principle on your mortgage
- the remaining principle on your student loans
- the remaining principle on your auto loans
- the remaining principle on your credit cards
- the remaining principle on your other debts

NET WORTH $

Subtract your debts from your possessions to determine your net worth. (If your debts exceed the value of your possessions, subtract your possessions from your debts and write a minus sign by your answer.)

YOUR SOCIAL SECURITY BENEFITS

To fully understand your financial needs, you should obtain an estimate of your Social Security benefits and copy them into the table below. Phone Social Security at 800-772-1213 and request a *Personal Earnings and Benefit Estimate Statement* for yourself and your spouse. Social Security will first send you a short form to complete.

When you receive the form, read this paragraph for assistance with Question 9. Question 9 asks you to predict your future earnings from jobs that pay into Social Security. If you plan to continue working steadily between now and retirement at such jobs, simply copy your answer from Question 7B of the form. Otherwise, estimate your average yearly earnings until retirement by predicting periods of unemployment, part-time work, or work at jobs paying more or less than your current training allows. **Do not** adjust future earnings for cost-of-living increases as the instructions indicate, because Social Security automatically assumes your income will rise with inflation.

Mail the form and allow six weeks to receive your statement. When it arrives, turn to page 3 of the statement and copy the numbers into the following table.

SOCIAL SECURITY BENEFITS

	You	Spouse
Monthly Retirement Benefits		
At full-retirement age	________	________
Monthly Survivor Benefits		
For your child	________	________
For your spouse who is caring for your child	________	________
When your spouse reaches full-retirement age	________	________
For all your family members, if others also qualify	________	________

Additional Information for Divorced or Widowed Singles

If you had a marriage lasting more than ten years that ended in divorce, or you had a marriage that ended in the death of your spouse, you might qualify for a larger retirement benefit than the one shown on your Social Security statement. However, before you investigate this possibility, note that you forfeit this larger benefit if you are married when you turn 60. So, if you think you might remarry before age 60, do not plan for this larger benefit.

If you *do* want to assume you will be eligible for this benefit, phone Social Security at 800-772-1213 and ask a representative to help you estimate your potential monthly retirement benefit from each former spouse. Record the largest value you obtain on the first blank under the heading Spouse in the table on the previous page.

Retirement Savings — Estimating Your Needs

This chapter provides instructions for using the retirement planning tools recommended on page 5. Instructions for the software begin below. Instructions for the workbook begin on page 57.

☐ Using the Software

To use the Fidelity software in conjunction with this book, follow these instructions as you work through **Module 2: Retirement Needs**.

Screen 1 simply introduces the module. Move to Screen 2 by selecting the right arrow button at the bottom right of the screen.

On **Screen 2** enter the information requested noting the following special instructions.

- **What is your current salary?**
  Into these cells enter your individual Gross Annual Incomes from page 50.

On **Screen 3** enter the information requested noting the following special instructions.

- **What is your annual retirement income goal?**
  This cell should already show a value equal to 70% of the total income you provided on Screen 2. Leave this value alone unless you want to do more detailed planning by selecting the button to the right of the cell.

  What is the significance of 70%? Experts suggest that you need between 60% and 80% of your current income (adjusted for inflation) to maintain your standard of living during retirement. Why not 100%? There are several reasons: you no longer need to save for retirement; you may have finished paying for your home; your children are probably grown; and you no longer have work expenses such as commuting and maintaining a professional wardrobe.

- **What will you receive annually from Social Security?**
  NOTE: If you enter a number in this cell and *then* select the button to its right, you lose your entry.

  If you are married . . .
  Plan to get only one set of benefits, even if you both expect to receive them. Here's why. Under current rules, your total benefits depend on how long each of you live. While you both live, you collect two sets of benefits.[1] However, upon a death, the surviving spouse collects only one set—roughly the larger set.

  If you obtained your Social Security statements, multiply the larger monthly At full-retirement age benefit recorded on page 52 by 12 and enter your answer in the cell in place of the estimate provided. If you do not have your Social Security statements, select the button to the

[1] You each receive the greater of your own benefit or half your spouse's.

right of the cell to display separate benefit estimates for each of you. Divide each estimate by 12 and enter your answers in the corresponding At full-retirement age blanks on page 52. Select *OK* to close the pop-up window. Now, multiply the larger monthly At full-retirement age benefit by 12 and enter your answer in the cell.

If you are divorced or widowed . . .
You might qualify for a former spouse's benefit instead of your own.[1] However, if you think you might remarry before age 60, do not rely on this benefit, but instead plan as though you are *single (never married)* described below.

If you *do* want to rely on this benefit, turn to page 52 and follow the instructions for obtaining the necessary Social Security information. Then multiply the greater of the two At full-retirement age monthly benefits you listed on page 52 by 12 and enter your answer in place of the estimate provided.

If you are single (never married) . . .
If you obtained your Social Security statement, multiply your monthly At full-retirement age benefit from page 52 by 12 and enter your answer in place of the estimate provided. If you do not have your Social Security statement, use the software's estimate. While the estimate is handy, divide it by 12 and enter your answer in the At full-retirement age blank on page 52.

On **Screen 4** enter the information requested noting the following special instructions.

- **How much have you saved so far in your retirement plan or other retirement accounts?**
  Select the button to the right of this cell to open a worksheet. If you own cash-value life insurance solely as a retirement investment, include the cash value with the value of your annuities.

- **How much have you saved toward retirement in accounts that are taxable?**
  If you have carefully earmarked some of your regular savings for retirement, select the button to the right of the cell to open a worksheet. Otherwise, leave the cell zero.

On **Screen 5** enter the information requested noting the following special instructions.

- **How much of your salary are you saving now per year?**
  THIS CELL SHOULD BE ZERO. The whole purpose of this analysis is to estimate your total annual savings needs. If you enter numbers here, you will confuse the results.

- **How much are your employer(s) contributing now per year?**
  THIS CELL SHOULD BE ZERO. Again, you are trying to estimate your total needs. Numbers here will confuse the results.

---

[1] You can receive the greater of (1) your own benefit, (2) your deceased spouse's benefit, (3) your divorced (now deceased) spouse's benefit if your marriage lasted more than ten years, or (4) half of your divorced (still living) spouse's benefit if your marriage lasted more than ten years. If you are married when you turn 60 you disqualify for benefits from former spouses.

Screen 6 shows you the results and lets you fiddle with the assumptions.

- **Inflation rate**
  Your savings estimates are extremely sensitive to inflation. Use the historical average inflation rate of 4% per year assumed in the software.
- **Return before retirement**
  Your savings estimates are extremely sensitive to the growth rate of your investments. Historically, long-term investments have returned roughly 9% to 11% per year on average. Change the 8% return suggested in the software to 9%, and select the *Calculate* button at the bottom of the screen.
- **Return after retirement**
  Your savings estimates are extremely sensitive to the growth rate of your investments. Historically, intermediate-term investments have returned roughly 7% to 9% per year on average. During retirement you should gradually shift your savings from long-term to intermediate-term investments. Assume an 8% return instead of the 7% suggested in the software. Again, select the *Calculate* button.
- **Your savings per year**
  THIS CELL SHOULD BE ZERO. This cell is a repeat from the previous screen. Again, the whole purpose of this analysis is to estimate your *total* savings needs.
- **Employer's contribution**
  THIS CELL SHOULD BE ZERO. This cell is also a repeat from the previous screen and should remain zero.
- **Additional annual savings required**
  Once you have decided on the assumptions you want to use, select the *Calculate* button and copy the number from this cell to line **A** of the table on page 7 of this book.

  If you need little or no savings . . .
  Do one or more of the following: plan for an early retirement by lowering your retirement age at the top of Screen 6; go back to Screen 3 and increase your retirement income goal; or go back to Screen 3 and reduce your reliance on Social Security.

  If you believe your savings needs are too large . . .
  Do one or both of the following: plan for a later retirement by raising your retirement age at the top of Screen 6; or assume you will work part time during retirement by returning to Screen 3 and selecting the button to the right of *What will you receive from pension and other sources?*

Save your file. If you altered the assumptions on Screen 6, jot down your changes because they are not saved with your file. You must re-enter these changes each time you open the file.

Congratulations! You have successfully estimated your retirement savings needs. Return to page 5 to read about where to save.

NOTE: **If you are married**, consider performing one more task before you leave the software. Turn to instruction **BB** on page 68 to estimate the life insurance needed to protect retirement income.

Using the Workbook

To use the T. Rowe Price workbook in conjunction with this book, follow these instructions as you work through Part One, STEPS 1 through 8. If you are married, make two photocopies of these workbook pages before you begin so you have blank versions available for assessing your life insurance needs.

Complete **STEPS 1** and **2** as instructed. (You can skip **Lines 18** and **19**.)

STEP 3 gives you two ways to set your income goal for retirement: a simple method and a detailed method. If you use the simple method, multiply your Net Annual Income (from the Total column on page 50) by 0.7 (70%), and enter your answer on **Line 21**.

What is the significance of 70%? Experts suggest that you need between 60% and 80% of your current income (adjusted for inflation) to maintain your standard of living during retirement. Why not 100%? There are several reasons: you no longer need to save for retirement; you may have finished paying for your home; your children are probably grown; and you no longer have work expenses such as commuting and maintaining a professional wardrobe.

Complete **STEP 4** noting the following special instructions.

- **Line 23** asks for your expected annual Social Security income.

  If you are married . . .
  Plan to get only one set of benefits, even if you both expect to receive them. Here's why. Under current rules, your total benefits depend on how long each of you live. While you both live, you collect two sets of benefits.[1] However, upon a death, the surviving spouse collects only one set—roughly the larger set.

  If you obtained your Social Security statements, multiply the larger monthly At full-retirement age benefit recorded on page 52 by 12 and enter your answer on Line 23 of the workbook. If you do not have your Social Security statements, use the workbook to estimate a *For Worker* benefit for each of you. (Do not use the *For Worker and Spouse* estimates.) Enter the larger estimate on Line 23 of the workbook. Also, while you have these numbers handy, divide them by 12 and enter your answers in the At full-retirement age blanks on page 52.

  If you are divorced or widowed . . .
  You might qualify for a former spouse's benefit instead of your own.[2] However, if you think you might remarry before age 60, do not rely on this benefit, but instead plan as though you are *single (never married)* described next.

  If you *do* want to rely on this benefit, turn to page 52 and follow the instructions for obtaining the necessary Social Security information. Then multiply the greater of the two At full-retirement age monthly

[1] You each receive the greater of your own benefit or half your spouse's.

[2] You can receive the greater of (1) your own benefit, (2) your deceased spouse's benefit, (3) your divorced (now deceased) spouse's benefit if your marriage lasted more than ten years, or (4) half of your divorced (still living) spouse's benefit if your marriage lasted more than ten years. If you are married when you turn 60 you disqualify for benefits from former spouses.

benefits you listed on page 52 by 12 and enter your answer on Line 23 of the workbook.

If you are single (never married) . . .
If you obtained your Social Security statement, multiply your monthly At full-retirement age benefit from page 52 by 12 and enter your answer on Line 23 of the workbook. If you do not have your Social Security statement, use the workbook to estimate your benefit. While this number is handy, divide it by 12 and enter your answer in the At full-retirement age blank on page 52.

Complete **STEP 5** as instructed.

Complete **STEP 6** noting the following special instructions.

- **Line 44** asks for the current value of your tax-deferred retirement savings. Include the value of variable annuities, and if you own cash-value life insurance solely as a retirement investment, include the cash values too.
- Skip **Lines 47** through **50** and enter zero on **Line 51**. These lines account for future employer contributions, but the whole purpose of this analysis is to estimate the total annual savings you need—including contributions from employers. If you enter a number other than zero on Line 51 you will confuse the results.

Complete **STEPS 7** and **8** as instructed. Copy the number from **Line 85** to line **A** of the table on page 7 of this book.

If you need little or no savings . . .
Redo the workbook planning for one or more of the following: an earlier retirement, a larger retirement income goal, or a reduced reliance on Social Security.

If you believe your savings needs are too large . . .
Redo the workbook planning for a later retirement or an income during retirement due to part-time employment.

Congratulations! You have successfully estimated your retirement savings needs. Return to page 5 to read about where to save.

NOTE: **If you are married**, consider performing one more task before you pack up the workbook. Turn to instruction **BB** on page 68 to estimate the life insurance needed to protect retirement income.

LIFE INSURANCE — ESTIMATING YOUR NEEDS

This chapter provides worksheets to help you estimate your life insurance needs. If you are single, begin working below. If you are married, begin working on page 64.

☐ Single

If you have children, or others who rely on your income, you may need life insurance to ensure that this income continues after your death. The amount of insurance you need depends on your specific financial responsibilities. Use the following worksheet to estimate your need.

NOTE: If you rely on alimony, child support, or other such income from a former partner, this income should be protected in case the former partner dies. Such protection may already be in place because it is often required under the terms of separation. However, if this protections is not in place, estimate the life insurance needed on a former partner by multiplying the annual income he or she provides by the number of years these payments will continue. Shop for this coverage when you shop for your own.

LIFE INSURANCE WORKSHEET — SINGLE

This worksheet helps you estimate your life insurance needs. Do not attempt to adjust your entries for cost-of-living increases or inflation. The worksheet already accounts for these.[1] If you do not have children under 18, begin with instruction **P**.

YEARS WITH CHILDREN UNDER 18

A Annual College Contribution
In column **A** on the next page, copy the Amount to save this year for each child from the table on page 13.

B Number of Contributions Remaining
In column **B**, enter the No. of years until college for each child from the table on page 13.

C Value of Remaining College Contributions (**A** x **B** for each child)
In column **C**, enter the value of your remaining contributions to college savings for each child. To determine these values, multiply the contribution **A** for each child by the number of contributions remaining **B** for each child.

[1] The worksheet assumes your *income* and *invested death benefits* grow at the rate of inflation. These assumptions simplify the worksheet significantly. The first assumption allows you to enter all future incomes in *today's dollars*. The second allows you to ignore the growth of death benefits invested for future use. This second assumption is probably conservative, because your investments may grow faster than inflation.

LIFE INSURANCE WORKSHEET — SINGLE

. . . continued

	A		B		C
Child 1	________	x	_____	=	__________
Child 2	________	x	_____	=	__________
Child 3	________	x	_____	=	__________
Child 4	________	x	_____	=	__________
Child 5	________	x	_____	=	__________

D Total Annual College Contribution — **D** __________ **(add column A)**

On line **D**, enter your total annual contribution to college savings for all children. To determine this value, add your annual contributions in column **A**.

E Total Value of Remaining College Contributions — **E** __________ **(add column C)**

On line **E**, enter the total value of your remaining contributions to college savings for all children. To determine this value, add your remaining contributions in column **C**.

F Years Until Children Are Grown — **F** __________

On line **F**, enter the number of years between now and the time your youngest child turns 18.

G Net Income — **G** __________

On line **G**, copy your Net Annual Income from page 50.

H Adjusted Net Income — **H** __________ **(G – D)**

Your contributions to college savings have the effect of lowering your net income while you raise children. To determine this adjusted net income, subtract your total annual college contribution **D** from your total net annual income **G**. Enter your answer on line **H**.

I Income Goal — **I** __________ **(H x 0.6)**

Experts suggest that a family is adequately protected if it can maintain between 60% and 80% of its income after the death of a provider. Because your children will enter another household that already covers its major expenses, plan to provide only 60% of your income to this new household until your children are grown. To determine your income goal, multiply your adjusted net income **H** by 0.6. Enter your answer on line **I**.

J Social Security Benefits — **J** __________

To determine how much life insurance you need to replace lost income, it is important to know how much other income the remaining family members will receive. This instruction and the next will help you estimate this income. Social Security can pay a substantial income to surviving family members. To estimate these benefits, complete the worksheet beginning on page 62 and record the results on line **J** above.

K Employer Pension Benefits — **K** __________

If you have a pension plan that will pay a steady income to your survivors, enter the annual amount of this benefit on line **K**. **Do not** include pension benefits that are paid in a lump sum because these benefits are recorded on line **S** of this worksheet.

LIFE INSURANCE WORKSHEET — SINGLE

. . . continued

L **Total Income Expected** — L ________ (J + K)

On line **L**, enter the total income your surviving family can expect from the previous two sources **J** and **K**.

M **Income Shortage** — M ________ (I – L) or zero

If the expected income **L** falls short of your goal **I**, subtract **L** from **I** and enter your answer on line **M**. Otherwise, enter zero on line **M** because there is no income shortage.

N **Insurance Needed** — N ________ (M x F)

On line **N**, enter the funds needed to remedy an income shortage. To determine this value, multiply the income shortage **M** by the number of years until your children are grown **F**.

COLLEGE SAVINGS

O **Insurance Needed** — O ________

Life insurance can completely fund college savings. On line **O**, copy the value of the total remaining college contributions **E**.

FINAL EXPENSES

P **Insurance Needed** — P ________

Make sure your funeral and other final expenses are covered. Enter $8,000 on line **P**.

DEBTS

Q **Insurance Needed** — Q ________

If your net worth (from page 51) is negative, enter it without the minus sign on line **Q**. If your net worth is positive, enter zero on line **Q**.

TOTALS

R **Total Insurance Needed** — R ________ (N + O + P + Q)

Add the insurance needs estimated above on lines **N**, **O**, **P**, and **Q**. Enter your answer on line **R**.

S **Employer-Paid Life Insurance** — S ________

If you want to rely on employer-paid life insurance, enter your coverage through work on line **S**. **Be sure to include any lump-sum death benefits from your pension plan.**

T **Net Worth** — T ________

If your net worth (from page 51) is positive, enter it on line **T**. If your net worth is negative, enter zero on line **T**.

U **Amount of Privately-Paid Life Insurance Needed** — U ________ (R – S – T)

Determine your need for privately-paid insurance by subtracting your employer-paid insurance **S** and your net worth **T** from your total insurance needed **R**. Round your answer up to the nearest $10,000, and enter it on line **U**. Turn to page 76 to shop for this coverage or to cancel unneeded policies.

SOCIAL SECURITY WORKSHEET — SINGLE

Complete the table on the next page if you are financially responsible for children or dependent adults.

This worksheet helps you estimate the Social Security benefits your family should receive if you die. Use the following instructions to complete the table on the next page.

Before you begin, you should note that certain situations disqualify survivors from receiving benefits. If either of the following situations apply to you, phone Social Security at 800-772-1213 and speak with a representative.

- SITUATION 1: If you are financially responsible for children other than your own, ask a Social Security representative to tell you which children will qualify for benefits if you die. As you complete this worksheet, only include children who will qualify.
- SITUATION 2: If you've worked very little, or if you plan to stop working soon, your employment record might not include enough work credits at the time of your death to qualify your survivors for benefits. Ask a Social Security representative to tell you how many work credits you have. If you have 40 or more, then qualification is assured. If you have fewer than 40 credits, ask the representative to help you determine if there will be a period between now and the time you return to work that your survivors won't qualify for benefits. If such a period will exist, you have two choices: you can either plan to work just enough to qualify, or you can plan to not rely on Social Security.

A **Benefit to Youngest Child**
In column **A** of the table on the next page, mark out the box that corresponds to the current age (rounded to the nearest birthday) of your youngest child. Then, mark out all of the boxes below this age. In each of the unmarked boxes, copy the <u>For your child</u> benefit from the table on page 52. If you did not obtain your Social Security statement, estimate the <u>For your child</u> benefit by multiplying your <u>At full-retirement age</u> benefit (shown in the same table) by 0.75. (You should have recorded this <u>At full-retirement age</u> value during your retirement planning using the software or workbook.)

B **Benefit to Second Youngest Child**
In column **B**, repeat instruction **A** for your second youngest child.

C **Benefit to Third Youngest Child**
In column **C**, repeat instruction **A** for your third youngest child.

D **Total**
In column **D**, mark out the same boxes you marked out in column **A**. Add the numbers in each row of **A**, **B**, and **C**, and enter your answers in column **D**. (If you support a dependent adult, phone Social Security at 800-772-1213 and ask a representative to tell you the monthly benefit to this adult if you die. Increase the values in each box of column **D** by the amount of this benefit.)

E **Family Maximum Benefit**
In column **E**, mark out the same boxes you marked out in column **A**. In each of the unmarked boxes, enter the <u>For all your family members, if others also qualify</u> benefit from the table on page 52. This value is also called the *family maximum*, and the total

SOCIAL SECURITY WORKSHEET — SINGLE
. . . continued

of your survivors' benefits cannot exceed this amount. If you did not obtain your Social Security statement, estimate the family maximum by multiplying your At full-retirement age benefit (shown in the same table) by 1.5.

F Actual Monthly Benefit
Compare the numbers in each row of columns **D** and **E**. Copy whichever number is smaller into column **F**.

G Monthly Total Benefit
Add the numbers in column **F**. Enter your answer in box **G**.

H Total Benefit
To determine the total benefit, multiply the monthly total benefit **G** by 12. Enter this number in box **H**.

I Social Security Benefit
To determine the average yearly Social Security benefit, divide the total benefit **H** by the number of years until your youngest child turns 18 (from line **F**, page 60). Enter your answer in box **I** below AND on line **J** of the Life Insurance Worksheet, page 60.

Child's Age	A	B	C	D	E	F
17						
16						
15						
14						
13						
12						
11						
10						
9						
8						
7						
6						
5						
4						
3						
2						
1						
0						

G	Monthly Total Benefit	(total of column **F**)	
H	Total Benefit	(**G** x 12)	
I	Social Security Benefit	(**H** ÷ **F** *from page 60*)	

☐ Married

If you have children, a spouse, or others who rely on your income, you may need life insurance to ensure that this income continues after your death. The amount of insurance you need depends on your specific financial responsibilities. Use the following worksheet to estimate this need for both you and your spouse.

NOTE: If you or your spouse relies on alimony, child support, or other such income from a former partner, this income should be protected in case the former partner dies. Such protection may already be in place because it is often required under the terms of separation. However, if this protections is not in place, estimate the life insurance needed on a former partner by multiplying the annual income he or she provides by the number of years these payments will continue. Shop for this coverage when you shop for your own.

LIFE INSURANCE WORKSHEET — MARRIED

This worksheet helps you estimate *your* need (denoted *you*) and *your spouse's* need (denoted *sps*) for privately-paid life insurance. Do not attempt to adjust your entries for cost-of-living increases or inflation. The worksheet already accounts for these.[1] If you do not have children under 18, begin with instruction **R**.

YEARS WITH CHILDREN UNDER 18

A Annual College Contribution
In column **A**, copy the Amount to save this year for each child from the table on page 13.

B Number of Contributions Remaining
In column **B**, enter the No. of years until college for each child from the table on page 13.

C Value of Remaining College Contributions (**A** x **B** for each child)
In column **C**, enter the value of your remaining contributions to college savings for each child. To determine these values, multiply the contribution **A** for each child by the number of contributions remaining **B** for each child.

	A		B		C
Child 1	________	x	______	=	__________
Child 2	________	x	______	=	__________
Child 3	________	x	______	=	__________
Child 4	________	x	______	=	__________
Child 5	________	x	______	=	__________

D Total Annual College Contribution **D** __________
On line **D**, enter your total annual contribution to college savings (add column **A**)
for all children. To determine this value, add your annual contributions in column **A**.

[1] The worksheet assumes your *incomes* and *invested death benefits* grow at the rate of inflation. These assumptions simplify the worksheet significantly. The first assumption allows you to enter all future incomes in *today's dollars*. The second allows you to ignore the growth of death benefits invested for future use. This second assumption is probably conservative, because your investments may grow faster than inflation.

LIFE INSURANCE WORKSHEET – MARRIED
. . . continued

E Total Remaining College Contributions E ________ **(add column C)**
On line **E**, enter the total value of your remaining contributions to college savings for all children. To determine this value, add your remaining contributions in column **C**.

F Years Until Children Are Grown F ________
On line **F**, enter the number of years between now and the time your youngest child turns 18.

G Net Income G ________
On line **G**, copy the Net Annual Income from the Total column on page 50.

H Adjusted Net Income H ________ **(G – D)**
Your contributions to college savings have the effect of lowering your net income while you raise children. To determine this adjusted net income, subtract your total annual college contribution **D** from your total net annual income **G**. Enter your answer on line **H**.

I Income Goal I ________ **(H x 0.8)**
Experts suggest that a family is adequately protected if it can maintain between 60% and 80% of its income after the death of a spouse. Plan to maintain 80% during years with children. To determine your income goal, multiply your adjusted net income **H** by 0.8. Enter your answer on line **I**.

J Surviving Spouse's Earnings **J***you* ________ **J***sps* ________
To determine how much insurance is needed to replace lost income, it is important to know how much other income the remaining family members will receive. This instruction and the next two will help you estimate this income. If *your spouse* expects to maintain his or her current level of income after your death, copy the Net Annual Income from the Spouse column on page 50 on line **J***you*. However, if your spouse expects to change his or her employment, such as returning to full-time work, enter your spouse's anticipated net earnings instead. **Do the same for yourself.** If you expect to maintain your current level of income after *your spouse's* death, enter the Net Annual Income for You from page 50 on line **J***sps*. Or, if you expect to change your employment, enter your anticipated net earnings instead.

K Social Security Benefits **K***you* ________ **K***sps* ________
Social Security can pay a substantial income to surviving family members. To estimate these benefits, complete the worksheet beginning on page 72 and record the results on line **K** above.

L Employer Pension Benefits **L***you* ________ **L***sps* ________
If *you* have a pension plan that will pay a steady income to your surviving spouse, enter the annual amount of this benefit on line **L***you*. **Do not** include pension benefits that are paid in a lump sum because these benefits are recorded on line **FF** of this worksheet. **Do the same for your spouse.** If *your spouse's* pension will pay *you* a steady income, enter the annual amount on line **L***sps*. Again, do not include pension benefits that are paid in a lump sum.

LIFE INSURANCE WORKSHEET — MARRIED

. . . continued

M Total Income Expected — **M***you* __________ (**J***you* + **K***you* + **L***you*) — **M***sps* __________ (**J***sps* + **K***sps* + **L***sps*)

On line **M**, enter the total income the surviving family can expect from the previous three sources.

N Income Shortage — **N***you* __________ (**I** – **M***you*) or zero — **N***sps* __________ (**I** – **M***sps*) or zero

If the expected income **M** falls short of your goal **I**, subtract **M** from **I** and enter your answer on line **N**. Otherwise, enter zero on line **N** because there is no income shortage.

O Insurance Needed — **O***you* __________ (**N***you* x **F**) — **O***sps* __________ (**N***sps* x **F**)

On line **O**, enter the funds needed to remedy an income shortage. To determine this value, multiply the income shortage **N** by the number of years until your children are grown **F**.

COLLEGE SAVINGS

P Can College Savings Contributions Continue? — **P***you*: Yes No — **P***sps*: Yes No

Annual contributions to college savings can continue if there is enough extra income. If the expected income **M** exceeds your goal **I**, the difference reveals excess income. If (**M***you* – **I**) is greater than the annual college contribution **D**, circle *Yes* for **P***you*. Otherwise, circle *No*. **Do the same for your spouse.** If (**M***sps* – **I**) is greater than **D**, circle *Yes* for **P***sps*. Otherwise, circle *No*.

Q Insurance Needed — **Q***you* __________ **E** or zero — **Q***sps* __________ **E** or zero

If the answer to **P***you* is *No*, use life insurance to completely fund college savings by entering the value of the total remaining college contributions **E** on line **Q***you*. Otherwise, enter zero. Also, if the answer to **P***sps* is *No*, enter the value from **E** on line **Q***sps*. Otherwise, enter zero.

YEARS BEFORE RETIREMENT WITHOUT CHILDREN UNDER 18

R Net Income — **R** __________

On line **R**, enter the Net Annual Income from the Total column on page 50 (or from instruction **G** on the previous page).

S Income Goal — **S** __________ (**R** x 0.6)

Experts suggest that a family is adequately protected if it can maintain between 60% and 80% of its income after the death of a spouse. To keep insurance costs down, plan to maintain 60% (or perhaps less if you both have good jobs). If you expect to support a dependent parent or an adult disabled child during these years, plan to maintain 80%. To determine your income goal, multiply your net income **R** by 0.6 (or 0.8 if appropriate). Enter your answer on line **S**.

T Surviving Spouse's Earnings — **T***you* __________ — **T***sps* __________

To determine how much insurance is needed to replace lost income, it is important to know how much other income the remaining family members will receive. This instruction and the next two will help you estimate this income. If *your spouse* expects to maintain his or her current level of income after your death, copy the Net Annual Income for your Spouse from page 50 on line **T***you*. However, if your spouse expects

LIFE INSURANCE WORKSHEET — MARRIED
. . . continued

to change his or her employment, such as returning to full-time work, enter your spouse's anticipated net earnings instead. **Do the same for yourself.** If you expect to maintain your current level of income after *your spouse's* death, copy the Net Annual Income for You from page 50 on line $\mathbf{T}_{sps}$. Or, if you expect to change your employment, enter your anticipated net earnings instead.

U Social Security Benefits — $\mathbf{U}_{you}$ ________ $\mathbf{U}_{sps}$ ________

Enter zeros on line **U** unless you or your spouse support a dependent parent or disabled child. If you do have such a dependent, phone Social Security at 1-800-772-1213 and ask a representative to help you estimate the monthly benefit if *you* die and the monthly benefit if *your spouse* dies. Multiply these monthly benefits by 12 and by the number of years you expect to receive these payments. Enter the results for *your* death on line $\mathbf{U}_{you}$ and those for *your spouse's* death on line $\mathbf{U}_{sps}$.

V Employer Pension Benefits — $\mathbf{V}_{you}$ ________ $\mathbf{V}_{sps}$ ________

If *you* have a pension plan that will pay a steady income to your surviving spouse, enter the annual amount of this benefit on line $\mathbf{V}_{you}$. (You may be able to copy the value from line **L** on page 65 if benefits don't change when your children are grown.) **Do not** include pension benefits that are paid in a lump sum because these benefits are recorded on line **FF** of this worksheet. **Do the same for your spouse.** If *your spouse's* pension will pay *you* a steady income, enter the annual amount on line $\mathbf{V}_{sps}$. Again, do not include pension benefits that are paid in a lump sum.

W Total Income Expected — $\mathbf{W}_{you}$ ________ $(\mathbf{T}_{you} + \mathbf{U}_{you} + \mathbf{V}_{you})$ $\mathbf{W}_{sps}$ ________ $(\mathbf{T}_{sps} + \mathbf{U}_{sps} + \mathbf{V}_{sps})$

Enter the total income the surviving family can expect from the above three sources.

X Income Shortage — $\mathbf{X}_{you}$ ________ $(\mathbf{S} - \mathbf{W}_{you})$ or zero $\mathbf{X}_{sps}$ ________ $(\mathbf{S} - \mathbf{W}_{sps})$ or zero

If the expected income **W** falls short of your goal **S**, subtract **W** from **S** and enter your answer on line **X**. Otherwise, enter zero on line **X** because there is no income shortage.

Y Years Until Surviving Spouse Retires — $\mathbf{Y}_{you}$ ________ $\mathbf{Y}_{sps}$ ________

On line $\mathbf{Y}_{you}$, enter the number of years between now and the time *your spouse* will retire. Also, on line $\mathbf{Y}_{sps}$, enter the number of years between now and the time *you* will retire.

Z Years to Protect — $\mathbf{Z}_{you}$ ________ $\mathbf{Y}_{you}$ or $(\mathbf{Y}_{you} - \mathbf{F})$ $\mathbf{Z}_{sps}$ ________ $\mathbf{Y}_{sps}$ or $(\mathbf{Y}_{sps} - \mathbf{F})$

If you do not have children under 18, simply copy the values from line **Y** to line **Z**. Otherwise, calculate the number of years between the time your youngest child turns 18 and retirement by subtracting **F** from **Y**.

AA Insurance Needed — $\mathbf{AA}_{you}$ ________ $(\mathbf{X}_{you} \times \mathbf{Z}_{you})$ $\mathbf{AA}_{sps}$ ________ $(\mathbf{X}_{sps} \times \mathbf{Z}_{sps})$

Enter the amount of life insurance needed to remedy an income shortage. To determine this value, multiply the income shortage **X** by the number of years to protect **Z**.

LIFE INSURANCE WORKSHEET — MARRIED

. . . continued

RETIREMENT

BB Insurance Needed **BB**$_{you}$ ___________ **BB**$_{sps}$ ___________

Life insurance can protect the surviving spouse's standard of living during retirement. You can estimate the insurance needed on *your* life and on *your spouse's* life by working through the retirement planning software or workbook two more times as instructed below. However, you might choose to enter zeros on line **BB**. Zeros are reasonable if the surviving spouse would consider remarriage, or if you are nearing retirement and already have most of your retirement savings tucked away.

> If the following software or workbook instructions involve more effort than you can muster, here's a simpler, less accurate method for estimating your needs.
>
> **Warning**: This method is likely to suggest far more insurance than you really need because it ignores or oversimplifies significant information. (For example, it does not account for the increased retirement benefits of a surviving spouse who returns to full-time work.)
>
> Multiply *your* employer's defined contribution **B**$_{you}$ (shown on page 7) by the number of years between now and your planned retirement. Enter your answer on line **BB**$_{you}$ above. **Do the same for your spouse.** Multiply *your spouse's* employer contribution **B**$_{sps}$ (again, from page 7) by the number of years between now and his or her planned retirement. Enter this answer on line **BB**$_{sps}$ above.

Instructions for Using the SOFTWARE

(1) Re-open your retirement file and save it as "SpouseIns.rtw". From the main screen, select **Module 2: Retirement Needs**. Move immediately to **Screen 3** and jot down the income goal shown at the top of the screen. (You may need to re-enter it later.)

(2) Go back to **Screen 2** and delete or set to zero all of the entries shown in the **Spouse** column.

(3) Move again to **Screen 3** and re-enter your original income goal in the top cell. Next, where it asks **What will you receive annually from Social Security?**, if you have your Social Security statements, enter 12 times whichever of the following monthly benefits is larger (shown on page 52): *your own* At full-retirement age benefit or *your spouse's* When your spouse reaches full-retirement age benefit. If you do not have your Social Security statements, enter 12 times whichever At full-retirement age benefit is larger.

(4) Again on **Screen 3**, if your spouse has a pension, select the button to the right of **What will you receive from pension and other sources?** and enter in the **You** column the benefit you expect during retirement if your spouse dies now.

(5) Skip to **Screen 6** without making changes to **Screens 4** and **5**. Make sure **Return before retirement** shows 9% and **Return after retirement** shows 8% if these were the values you used for your original retirement calculation. Press *Calculate*.

LIFE INSURANCE WORKSHEET — MARRIED

. . . continued

(6) Go back to **Screen 5** and select the button to the right of **How much of your salary are you saving now per year?** In the **You** column of the pop-up window, enter the amount you expect to be able to contribute after the death of your spouse. The **Spouse** column should show zeros. Select *OK* when you are finished.

(7) Also on **Screen 5**, press the button to the right of **How much are your employer(s) contributing now per year?** In the **You** column of the pop-up window, enter the employer contribution you expect after the death of your spouse. The **Spouse** column should show zeros. Again, select *OK* when you are finished.

(8) Select *Calculate* at the bottom of **Screen 5**. A pop-up window will appear. Multiply the value shown for **Thus you'll need to accumulate an additional nest egg of** by the factor (shown below) that corresponds to the number of years until *you* retire. Copy your answer into blank **BB**$_{sps}$ on the previous page, and save your file.

yrs	factor	yrs	factor	yrs	factor	yrs	factor	yrs	factor	yrs	factor	yrs	factor
50	0.087	43	0.123	36	0.173	29	0.243	22	0.342	15	0.481	8	0.677
49	0.092	42	0.129	35	0.181	28	0.255	21	0.359	14	0.505	7	0.711
48	0.096	41	0.135	34	0.190	27	0.268	20	0.377	13	0.530	6	0.746
47	0.101	40	0.142	33	0.200	26	0.281	19	0.396	12	0.557	5	0.784
46	0.106	39	0.149	32	0.210	25	0.295	18	0.416	11	0.585	4	0.823
45	0.111	38	0.157	31	0.220	24	0.310	17	0.436	10	0.614	3	0.864
44	0.117	37	0.164	30	0.231	23	0.326	16	0.458	9	0.645	2	0.907

(9) Re-open your original retirement file and save it as "YourIns.rtw". Step through each screen of **Module 2: Retirement Needs** and swap the values for you and your spouse (because the software does not allow you to remove information in the **You** column).

(10) Move to **Screen 2** and delete or set to zero all of the entries shown in the **Spouse** column.

(11) Move to **Screen 3** and re-enter your original income goal in the top cell. Next, where it asks **What will you receive annually from Social Security?**, if you have your Social Security statements, enter 12 times whichever of the following monthly benefits is larger (shown on page 52): your spouse's At full-retirement age benefit or your own When your spouse reaches full-retirement age benefit. If you do not have your Social Security statements, enter 12 times whichever At full-retirement age benefit is larger.

(12) Again on **Screen 3**, if *you* have a pension, select the button to the right of **What will you receive from pension and other sources?** and enter in the **You** column the benefit your spouse should expect during retirement if you die now.

(13) Skip to **Screen 6** without making changes to **Screens 4** and **5**. Make sure **Return before retirement** shows 9% and **Return after retirement** shows 8% if these were the values you used for your original retirement calculation. Press *Calculate.*

(14) Go back to **Screen 5** and select the button to the right of **How much of your salary are you saving now per year?** In the **You** column of the pop-up window, enter the amount your spouse should be able to contribute after your death. The **Spouse** column should show zeros. Select *OK* when you are finished.

LIFE INSURANCE WORKSHEET — MARRIED

... continued

(15) Also on **Screen 5**, press the button to the right of **How much are your employer(s) contributing now per year?** In the **You** column of the pop-up window, enter the employer contribution your spouse expects after your death. The **Spouse** column should show zeros. Again, select *OK* when you are finished.

(16) Select *Calculate* at the bottom of **Screen 5**. A pop-up window will appear. Multiply the value shown for **Thus you'll need to accumulate an additional nest egg of** by the factor (shown on the previous page) that corresponds to the number of years until your spouse retires. Copy your answer into blank **BB***you* on page 68, and save your file.

(If you turned to these instructions during your retirement planning, go back to page 5 to read about where to save for retirement.)

Instructions for Using the WORKBOOK

Perform the following set of instructions twice. The first time, estimate *your* life insurance needs by assuming that *you* have died as you complete a copy of the workbook. The second time, estimate *your spouse's* needs by assuming *he* or *she* has died.

(1) Some of the numbers you entered during your retirement planning can simply be transferred to the new copy of the workbook. Copy the values for Lines 1 – 6, 8, 9, 10, 21 or 22, 24, 27, 30, 33, 38, 39, 40, 44, 53, 55, 72, and 73.

(2) Review the following lines for possible changes from your original retirement planning workbook.

- Line 7 Enter the number of years until retirement for the surviving spouse.
- Line 11 Enter the expected number of retirement years for the surviving spouse.
- Line 20 If Lines 7 and 11 indicate that the surviving spouse is no longer planning an early retirement, this factor will change.
- Line 23 If you have your Social Security statements, enter 12 times whichever of the following monthly benefits is larger (shown on page 52): the At full-retirement age benefit for the surviving spouse or the When your spouse reaches full-retirement age benefit shown for the deceased. If you do not have your Social Security statements, enter 12 times whichever At full-retirement age benefit is larger.
- Line 26 Pension benefits during retirement might change after the death of a spouse.
- Line 29 Sources of other income during retirement might change after the death of a spouse.
- Line 47 **Do not follow the directions in the workbook.** Instead, enter the total annual contribution the surviving spouse expects from all sources. Definitely include employer contributions with matching. Also include personal contributions to retirement by the surviving spouse if they would be affordable.
- Line 77 Sources of other capital (such as an inheritance to the deceased) might change after the death of a spouse.

(3) Go back to the beginning of the workbook and fill in the remaining lines up through Line 83. If this is your first time through these instructions, you should be

LIFE INSURANCE WORKSHEET — MARRIED

. . . continued

estimating *your* life insurance needs. Copy the value from Line 83 to line **BB***you* on page 68. If this is your second time through, you should be estimating *your spouse's* life insurance needs and copy the value from Line 83 to line **BB***sps*.

(If you turned to these instructions during your retirement planning, go back to page 5 to read about where to save for retirement.)

FINAL EXPENSES

CC Insurance Needed CC*you* ________ CC*sps* ________

Make sure that funeral and other final expenses are covered for you and your spouse. Enter $8,000 in both blanks.

OTHER

DD Insurance Needed DD*you* ________ DD*sps* ________

Your death or your spouse's death may generate additional expenses, such as child care, transportation, cleaning, or tax preparation. Estimate the annual value of *your* services that your spouse would not perform in your absence. Then multiply these values by the number of years these services would be needed. Enter the total value on line **DD***you*. For example, four years of full-time child care at $10,000 per year would amount to $40,000 of additional insurance. **Do the same for your spouse.** Estimate the annual value of *your spouse's* services that *you* would not perform in his or her absence. Multiply these values by the number of years these services would be needed. Enter the total value on line **DD***sps*. **Describe these expenses at the bottom of page 84.**

TOTALS

EE Total Insurance Needed EE*you* ________ EE*sps* ________

Add the insurance needed for each spouse, and enter the results in the blanks.

EE*you* = (**O***you* + **Q***you* + **AA***you* + **BB***you* + **CC***you* + **DD***you*), and

EE*sps* = (**O***sps* + **Q***sps* + **AA***sps* + **BB***sps* + **CC***sps* + **DD***sps*).

FF Employer-Paid Life Insurance FF*you* ________ FF*sps* ________

If you want to rely on employer-paid life insurance, enter *your* coverage through work on line **FF***you* and *your spouse's* coverage on line **FF***sps*. **Be sure to include any lump-sum death benefits from a pension plan.**

GG Savings GG*you* ________ GG*sps* ________

Savings are the most economical form of protection when insurance needs are small. On line **GG***you*, enter the savings you will use to offset *your* life insurance needs. On line **GG***sps*, enter the savings you will use to offset *your spouse's* life insurance needs.

HH Amount of Privately-Paid Life Insurance Needed

Determine your needs for privately-paid insurance by subtracting employer-paid insurance **FF** and savings **GG** from the total insurance need **EE**. Round your answers up to the nearest $10,000, and enter them below. Turn to page 76 to shop for this coverage or to cancel unneeded policies.

HH*you* ________ **HH***sps* ________

(**EE***you* – **FF***you* – **GG***you*) (**EE***sps* – **FF***sps* – **GG***sps*)

SOCIAL SECURITY WORKSHEET — MARRIED

Complete the tables on pages 74 and 75 if you are financially responsible for children or dependent adults.

This worksheet helps you estimate the Social Security benefits paid to your family if you or your spouse should die. The worksheet ends in two identical tables—one for you and one for your spouse. Use the following instructions to complete the tables.

Before you begin, you should note that certain situations disqualify survivors from receiving benefits. If either of the following situations apply to you, phone Social Security at 1-800-772-1213 and speak with a representative.

- SITUATION 1: If you or your spouse are financially responsible for children who are not your own, ask a Social Security representative to tell you which children will qualify for benefits if *you* die, and which children will qualify if *your spouse* dies. As you complete these worksheets, only include children who will qualify.
- SITUATION 2: If you or your spouse have worked very little, or plan to stop working soon, your employment record might not include enough work credits at the time of your death to qualify your survivors for benefits. Ask a Social Security representative to tell you how many work credits you each have. If you both have 40 or more, then qualification is assured. If one of you has fewer than 40 credits, ask the representative to help you determine if there will be a period between now and the time you return to work that your survivors won't qualify for benefits. If such a period will exist, you have two choices: you can either plan to work just enough to qualify, or you can plan to not rely on Social Security.

A Benefit to Youngest Child
In column **A***you*, mark out the box that corresponds to the current age (rounded to the nearest birthday) of *your* youngest child. Then, mark out all of the boxes below this age. In each of the unmarked boxes, copy the For your child benefit from the You column of the table on page 52. If you do not have your Social Security statement, estimate the For your child by multiplying your At full-retirement age benefit (shown in the same table) by 0.75. (You should have recorded this At full-retirement age benefit during your retirement planning using the software or workbook.) **Do the same for your spouse.** In column **A***sps*, mark out the box that corresponds to the current age of *your spouse's* youngest child. Then, mark out all of the boxes below this age. In each of the unmarked boxes, copy the For your child benefit from the Spouse column of the table on page 52. Again, if your spouse does not have a Social Security statement, estimate the For your child benefit by multiplying his or her At full-retirement age benefit (shown in the same table) by 0.75.

B Benefit to Second Youngest Child
In columns **B***you* and **B***sps*, repeat instruction **A** for the second youngest child.

C Benefit to Third Youngest Child
In columns **C***you* and **C***sps*, repeat instruction **A** for the third youngest child.

D Benefit to Surviving Spouse
In column **D***you*, mark out the same boxes you marked out in column **A***you*. (Note that the boxes for ages 16 and 17 are also marked out, because a surviving spouse can only receive Social Security benefits through age 15 of the youngest child.) If your

SOCIAL SECURITY WORKSHEET — MARRIED

. . . continued

surviving spouse will work after your death, write zeros in the unmarked boxes.[1] Otherwise, copy the For your spouse who is caring for your child benefit from the You column of the table on page 52 into each unmarked box. If you do not have your Social Security statement, estimate this benefit by multiplying your At full-retirement age benefit (shown in the same table) by 0.75. **Do the same for your spouse.** In column $\mathbf{D}_{sps}$, mark out the same boxes you marked out in column $\mathbf{A}_{sps}$. If *you* plan to work after your spouse's death, write zeros in the unmarked boxes. Otherwise, copy the For your spouse who is caring for your child benefit from the Spouse column of the table on page 52 into each unmarked box. Again, if your spouse does not have a Social Security statement, estimate this benefit by multiplying his or her At full-retirement age benefit (shown in the same table) by 0.75.

E Total
In column $\mathbf{E}_{you}$, mark out the same boxes you marked out in column $\mathbf{A}_{you}$. In column $\mathbf{E}_{sps}$, mark out the same boxes you marked out in column $\mathbf{A}_{sps}$. Add the numbers in each row of **A**, **B**, **C**, and **D**, and enter the results in column **E**. **If you support a dependent adult**, phone Social Security at 1-800-772-1213 and ask a representative to tell you the monthly benefit to them *if you die* and *if your spouse dies*. Increase the values in each box of column $\mathbf{E}_{you}$ by the benefit from *your* death, and the values in column $\mathbf{E}_{sps}$ by the benefit from *your spouse's* death.

F Family Maximum Benefit
In column $\mathbf{F}_{you}$, mark out the same boxes you marked out in column $\mathbf{A}_{you}$. In each of the unmarked boxes, enter the For all your family members, if others also qualify benefit from the You column of the table on page 52. This value is also called the *family maximum*, and the total of your survivors' benefits cannot exceed this amount. If you do not have your Social Security statement, estimate the family maximum by multiplying your At full-retirement age benefit (shown in the same table) by 1.5. **Do the same for your spouse.** In column $\mathbf{F}_{sps}$, mark out the same boxes you marked out in column $\mathbf{A}_{sps}$. In each of the unmarked boxes, enter the For all your family members, if others also qualify benefit from the Spouse column of the table on page 52. Again, if your spouse does not have a Social Security statement, estimate the family maximum by multiplying his or her At full-retirement age benefit (shown in the same table) by 1.5.

G Actual Monthly Benefit
Compare the numbers in each row of columns **E** and **F**. Copy whichever number is smaller into column **G**.

H Monthly Total Benefit
Add the numbers in column **G**, and enter the result in box **H**.

[1] This is a conservative assumption, because a working spouse can actually receive a benefit. However, this benefit begins to phase out once the surviving spouse's income exceeds roughly $10,000 per year.

SOCIAL SECURITY WORKSHEET – MARRIED

. . . continued

I Total Benefit
To determine the total benefit, multiply the monthly total benefit **H** by 12. Enter this number in box **I**.

J Social Security Benefit
To determine the average yearly Social Security benefit after *your* death, divide the total benefit **I***you* by the number of years until your youngest child turns 18 (from line **F**, page 65). Enter the result in box **J***you*. **Do the same for your spouse.** Divide the total benefit **I***sps* by **F** and enter the result in box **J***sps*. Copy the value for **J***you* to line **K***you* and the value for **J***sps* to line **K***sps* of the Life Insurance Worksheet, page 65.

Child's Age	**A***you*	**B***you*	**C***you*	**D***you*	**E***you*	**F***you*	**G***you*
17				XXXXX			
16				XXXXX			
15							
14							
13							
12							
11							
10							
9							
8							
7							
6							
5							
4							
3							
2							
1							
0							

H*you*	Monthly Total Benefit	(total of column **G***you*)	
I*you*	Total Benefit	(**H***you* x 12)	
J*you*	Social Security Benefit	(**I***you* ÷ **F** *from page 65*)	

SOCIAL SECURITY WORKSHEET — MARRIED

. . . continued

Child's Age	**A***sps*	**B***sps*	**C***sps*	**D***sps*	**E***sps*	**F***sps*	**G***sps*
17				XXXXX			
16				XXXXX			
15							
14							
13							
12							
11							
10							
9							
8							
7							
6							
5							
4							
3							
2							
1							
0							

H*sps*	Monthly Total Benefit	(total of column **G***sps*)	
I*sps*	Total Benefit	(**H***sps* x 12)	
J*sps*	Social Security Benefit	(**I***sps* ÷ **F** *from page 65*)	

LIFE INSURANCE — SHOPPING INSTRUCTIONS

This chapter provides step-by-step instructions to help you find quality, low-cost life insurance.

☐ STEP 1: Inventory Your Existing Policies

Record your current coverages in the table below. Only include insurance that *you* pay for. (For instance, *do not* include employer-paid insurance, but *do* include insurance that *you* pay for through your employer.) Make sure you record annual premiums. Be sure to list all of your term and cash-value policies. Also include mortgage insurance if you have it. If your premiums change each year for certain policies, simply list the current year's premium and place an asterisk by it. Later, this table will help you decide which policies to keep and which to cancel.

LIFE INSURANCE INVENTORY					
You			*Spouse*		
Policy Type & Company	**Annual Premium** ($ per year)	**Death Benefit** ($)	**Policy Type & Company**	**Annual Premium** ($ per year)	**Death Benefit** ($)
*insurance **you** pay for through your employer*			*insurance **you** pay for through your employer*		
TOTALS			**TOTALS**		

☐ STEP 2: Record the Amount of Life Insurance You Need

On the Death Benefit line of the shopping list on page 79, write the values from page 71, line **HH** if you are married. If you are single, write the value from page 61, line **U**.

☐ STEP 3: Select a Policy Type

There are two kinds of life insurance: term and cash-value. **Term insurance** is pure life insurance. **Cash-value insurance** combines term insurance with a savings plan making it an impractical form of life insurance. (Cash-value is a generic name for the set of products that includes *whole life*, *ordinary life*, *universal life*, *variable life*, *variable universal life*, *adjustable life*, *single-premium life*, and others.)

There are two types of term life insurance to consider:

- **Level premium term**: Your coverage and premium remain constant for the duration of the policy. These policies are a good value, and premiums are simple to compare.
- **Annual renewable term**: Your coverage remains constant, but your premium increases each year. These policies are a good value, but premiums are often difficult to compare.

In the shopping list on page 79, write in the Policy Type you want. The remainder of this chapter assumes you will shop for term insurance.

☐ STEP 4: Select Policy Features

The following table describes policy features for term life insurance. Read about the features and write your selections in the shopping list on page 79. For your convenience, the shopping list shows the recommended features in italics.

FEATURES — LIFE INSURANCE	
Description	*Recommendation*
Term: The term specifies the number of years the policy is in force. 1, 5, 10, 15, and 20 years are the standard increments.	Choose 5 or 10 year term (10 year term is more convenient). *Annual renewable term* is a good value, but premiums are difficult to compare. 15 and 20 year term policies are too expensive because your coverage needs should fall as you age.
Renewable: The insurer must let you renew your policy at the end of the term, regardless of your health. This right ends at the age specified by the policy, typically 65 or older.	This feature is critical. Without it, you might not be able to get insurance when you need it. Make sure your policy is renewable to at least age 65.

FEATURES — LIFE INSURANCE . . . continued	
Description	*Recommendation*
Re-entry : The insurer may evaluate your health when renewing your policy. Re-entry policies allow you to pay lower premiums for as long as you are in good health.	Shop for policies without regard to the re-entry provision. STEP 7 will help you compare policies with and without re-entry.
Cost-of-Living Rider: This rider allows your coverage to rise with inflation. *OR* **Guaranteed Insurability Rider**: This rider gives you the ability to purchase additional coverage without proving insurability. The policy limits the amount of coverage you can buy and when you can buy it.	Do not purchase this rider, because your insurance needs estimated in this book already account for inflation. Do not purchase this rider for two reasons. First, your insurance needs will likely decrease with time. And second, to make this rider pay off you must become uninsurable, otherwise you can simply purchase additional coverage when you need it.
Convertibility Rider: This rider lets you convert your insurance to a cash-value policy without proving insurability. This feature allows you to carry life insurance late into your retirement years.	Do not purchase this rider, because your need for life insurance should end by retirement. (Many policies include this rider at no extra cost.)
Waiver of Premium Rider: If you become disabled, the insurance company will pay your life insurance premiums for you.	Do not purchase this rider. It overlaps your disability protection, and benefits depend on the policy's definition of disability.
Accidental Death Rider (sometimes called **Double Indemnity**) : Your death benefit is increased if you die in an accident.	Do not purchase this rider, because your need for coverage does not depend on *how* you die.
Children's Protection Rider: This rider insures the lives of your children.	Do not purchase this rider, because children do not need life insurance.

☐ STEP 5: Choose Where to Shop

Let the following quote services do your shopping. Quote services are the most convenient way to shop. They search hundreds of policies for you, and then mail you quotes for the lowest priced policies they can sell you. There is no pressure, no obligation, no cost, and you never meet with an insurance agent.

InsuranceQuote	800-972-1104	MasterQuote	800-337-5433
Jack White & Co.	800-622-3699	Quotesmith	800-556-9393
LifeQuote	800-521-7873	SelectQuote	800-343-1985
LifeRates	800-457-2837	TermQuote	800-444-8376

☐ **STEP 6: Shop** (**Do not buy or cancel any policies in this step.**)

As you make your phone calls, use the following table to help you describe the policies you want. Ask that your quotes include the *guaranteed rates.* (Guaranteed rates are described in STEP 7.)

If you find that you cannot get coverage through a private insurance company, call your state's insurance department to learn if you have other options for obtaining coverage. (Some states operate risk-sharing pools.)

SHOPPING LIST — LIFE INSURANCE

For your convenience, the recommendations of this book are provided in italics.

	You	Spouse
Death Benefit	$__________	$__________
Policy Type		
level premium term	__________	__________
Policy Features		
10 year term	__________	__________
renewable to age 65	__________	__________
	__________	__________
	__________	__________
	__________	__________

☐ **STEP 7: Compare the Quotes**

Discard all policies that are not renewable. (*Renewable* is defined on page 77.) Convert all monthly and semi-annual quotes to annual values so you can compare the policies easily.

Policies that offer re-entry quote two sets of premiums. (*Re-entry* is defined on page 78.) If you remain healthy, you pay the lower set of premiums. If you become unhealthy, you pay no more than the higher set (called the **guaranteed rates**). Policies that *do not* offer re-entry quote a single set of premiums that you pay regardless of your health. Separate the policies into two groups: those that offer re-entry and those that do not. Find the two or three least expensive policies of each type and compare their descriptions closely. Rank your final selections.

☐ **STEP 8: Compare Your Selections to Your Existing Policies** (**Do not buy or cancel any policies in this step.**)

To compare policies having different death benefits, use the following formula to calculate the cost per $1,000 of coverage. Here's an example.

Which of the following policies is cheaper? Policy A costs $300 per year and provides $250,000 of coverage. Policy B costs $200 per year and provides $150,000 of coverage. The answer is Policy A, which costs $1.20 for each $1,000 of coverage, whereas Policy B costs $1.33 per $1,000 of coverage.

$$\text{cost per \$1,000 of coverage} = \$1{,}000 \times \left(\frac{\text{premium}}{\text{death benefit}}\right)$$

It is difficult to perform this calculation for a cash-value policy due to its savings component. For instance, you may have a whole life policy that appears to be free because you are not asked to pay premiums. In this case, the savings portion of the policy is earning enough interest each year to pay your premiums. STEP 9 explains alternatives for handling your cash-value life insurance.

☐ STEP 9: Decide If You Will Keep Existing Policies (Do not buy or cancel any policies in this step.)

If after reading the following passages you decide to keep any of your existing policies, reduce the Death Benefit (in the shopping list on the previous page) by subtracting the death benefits of the policies you will keep. Then return to STEP 6 to shop for this lower coverage.

Consider cancelling insurance that *you* pay for through your employer. If you leave your job, you may have to cancel this coverage or convert it to an expensive cash-value policy. Read your employer's policy carefully.

If you have mortgage insurance, plan to cancel it. (Mortgage insurance is an expensive form of life insurance that pays the remainder of your mortgage if you die.) You do not need this coverage if you calculated your insurance needs using the worksheet (page 59).

If you own a cash-value life insurance policy, here are several things you can do.

Option A: Keep the policy.
Choose this option in the following cases:

- you have become uninsurable and need the coverage; OR
- the policy will become part of your retirement plan.

Option B: Cancel the policy and transfer the cash value to an annuity.
Choose this option if you plan to keep or purchase an annuity as part of your retirement savings. A transfer to an annuity protects the tax-deferred earnings. Page 105 will help you find a quality, low-cost annuity. To avoid the taxes, you cannot perform this transfer yourself. Ask the annuity company to handle it.

Option C: Cancel the policy and collect the cash value.
Choose this option in all other cases. You *do* pay the income taxes you've been avoiding up to this point, but the taxable earnings are often only a small portion of the cash value. Also, the federal and state governments do not penalize withdrawals before age 59½ for most types of cash-value life insurance. If you are only a few years from retiring and expect your tax bracket to fall at that time, wait until then to cancel your policy.

Options B and C might appear unattractive when you note the size of your insurance policy's surrender charge. Can the performance of an alternative investment offset this charge? This question is difficult to answer because cash-value insurance is a complicated combination of life insurance and savings. To get an answer, you must try to separate these components and compare them individually to term life insurance and an alternative investment. For $40, the Consumer Federation of America will perform this comparison for you. Phone 202-387-6124 (or write 1424 16th St. NW, Suite 604, Washington, DC 20036) and ask for an information sheet.

☐ STEP 10: Check Insurance Company Ratings

Use the advice on page 98 to help you evaluate the financial strength of your proposed and existing insurance companies.

☐ STEP 11: Purchase the New Insurance

(Do not cancel any policies in this step.)

If the insurance company approves your application, check to see that the premium matches the original quote. If the premium has increased, do not accept the policy. Instead, ask the company to explain the increase, and then apply for coverage from several other insurers. If the companies seem to agree that you are more expensive to insure, return to STEP 8 and compare these new quotes to your existing policies.

When you purchase new coverage, reduce your premium by paying it annually instead of more frequently. If you are accustomed to paying your premium in monthly installments, be sure to budget for this annual payment.

☐ STEP 12: Cancel Your Unneeded Insurance

(Make sure your new policies are in force before cancelling any insurance.)

Read your existing policies carefully to determine *how* and *when* to cancel them. Some policies terminate automatically when you stop paying the premiums, while others require a written request for cancellation. Some policies refund part of your premium when you cancel mid-year, while others do not. If you will not get a refund for a mid-year cancellation, wait until the end of the policy year to cancel.

Life Insurance — Managing Benefits

This chapter provides instructions for managing life insurance benefits to ensure they deliver their intended protection. If the deceased was single, begin reading below. If married, begin on the next page.

☐ Single

In the event of your death, the person handling your estate should:

(1) Notify Social Security at 800-772-1213 so that survivors may begin collecting benefits.

(2) Request that insurance benefits be paid in a lump sum (instead of installments) so that they may be invested according to the instructions below.

The following passages suggest how to allocate and manage funds from the estate. Note that the overall value of the estate has probably changed since the time this plan was enacted, and that certain financial needs may have changed.

Years With Children Under 18 $__________

Turn to page 61 and copy the value from line **N** onto the blank above. This value represents the amount of money needed to supply income during the years there are children to raise.

Invest this money in mutual funds. (Refer to page 99 for information about mutual funds.) To generate a steady income from this money, ask the mutual fund company to set up the account for monthly systematic withdrawals. Set the amount of each withdrawal equal to the total value of the account divided by the number of months until the youngest child turns 18. Be sure to recompute this withdrawal once a year to ensure that the money does not run out early.

College Savings $__________

Turn to page 61 and copy the value from line **O** onto the blank above. This value represents the amount of money that should be devoted to college savings for the children. Refer to page 12 for information about saving for college.

Final Expenses $__________

Turn to page 61 and copy the value from line **P** onto the blank above. This value represents the amount of money available to cover final expenses.

Debts $__________

Turn to page 61 and copy the value from line **Q** onto the blank above. This value represents the amount of money needed to cover debts at the time the worksheet was completed.

☐ Married

If your spouse has died, do the following:

(1) Use emergency savings to cover current expenses.

(2) Make sure your spouse's retirement savings remain invested for *your* retirement.

(3) Notify Social Security at 800-772-1213 so that you may begin collecting benefits.

(4) Request that insurance benefits be paid in a lump sum (instead of installments) so that they may be invested according to the instructions below.

The following passages suggest how to allocate and manage your spouse's life insurance benefits. Be alert for financial needs that may have changed since the time this plan was enacted.

Turn to page 2 and note which label—*you* or *sps*—corresponds to the deceased spouse. The following passages will ask you to copy numbers from the worksheet beginning on page 64. Copy only those numbers having the deceased spouse's label.

Years With Children Under 18 $___________

Turn to page 66 and copy the appropriate value from line **O** onto the blank above. This value represents the amount of money needed to supply income during the years you are raising children.

Invest this money in mutual funds. (Refer to page 99 for information about mutual funds.) To receive a steady income from this money, ask your mutual fund company to set up your account for monthly systematic withdrawals. Set the amount of each withdrawal equal to the total value of your account divided by the number of months until your youngest child turns 18. Be sure to recompute this withdrawal once a year to ensure that the money does not run out early.

Instead of investing this money in mutual funds, you may be able to completely pay off the mortgage on your home. This strategy has the effect of increasing your income because it eliminates your monthly mortgage payment. However, consider your situation carefully, because the interest you pay on your mortgage is tax-deductible.

College Savings $___________

Turn to page 66 and copy the appropriate value from line **Q** onto the blank above. This value represents the amount of money you should devote to college savings for your children. Refer to page 12 for information about saving for college.

Years Before Retirement Without Children Under 18 $___________

Turn to page 67 and copy the appropriate value from line **AA** onto the blank above. This value represents the amount of money needed to supply income during the years before retirement when you are not raising children.

Invest this money in mutual funds. (Refer to page 99 for information about mutual funds.) When your youngest child turns 18, ask your mutual fund company to set up your account for monthly systematic withdrawals. Set the amount of each withdrawal equal to the total value of your account divided by the number of months until you retire. Be sure to recompute this withdrawal once a year to ensure that the money does not run out early.

Instead of investing this money in mutual funds, you may be able to pay down the mortgage on your home. This strategy can end your monthly mortgage payments either now, or by the time your youngest child reaches 18. However, consider your situation carefully, because the interest you pay on your mortgage is tax-deductible.

Retirement $__________

Turn to page 68 and copy the appropriate value from line **BB** onto the blank above. This value represents the amount of money you should contribute to your retirement savings.

If the amount is small and you are a disciplined saver, invest this money in your employer retirement plan or IRA over the next few years to take advantage of tax-deductible contributions. Otherwise, invest the full amount directly into an annuity or into stock mutual funds outside of a retirement account. Refer to page 4 for information about retirement savings.

Final Expenses $__________

Turn to page 71 and copy the appropriate value from line **CC** onto the blank above. This value represents the amount of money available to cover final expenses.

Other $__________

Turn to page 71 and copy the appropriate value from line **DD** onto the blank above. This value represents the amount of money available to cover the expenses described below.

____

____

____

____

____

____

____

____

____

____

____

Disability Insurance — Shopping Instructions

This chapter provides step-by-step instructions to help you find quality, low-cost disability insurance.

☐ STEP 1: Record the Amount of Coverage You Need

Copy your Amount of Privately-Paid Disability Insurance Needed from line **I** on page 26 into the Coverage line of the shopping list on page 88.

☐ STEP 2: Select a Policy Type

There are two types of disability insurance:

- **Level premium disability**: Your premium remains constant.
- **Renewable term disability**: Your premium changes each time the policy renews. (Policies normally renew annually or every 5 years.)

Choose a renewable term policy to take advantage of lower premiums during the early years of coverage. This strategy pays off if you eventually get better coverage through an employer so you can reduce or eliminate your private insurance. Enter a Policy Type in the shopping list on page 88.

☐ STEP 3: Select Policy Features

The following table describes disability policy features. Read about the features and write your selections in the shopping list on page 88. For your convenience, the shopping list shows the recommended features in italics.

FEATURES — DISABILITY INSURANCE	
Description	*Recommendation*
Noncancelable OR **Guaranteed Renewable**: The insurer must let you renew your policy at the end of the policy period regardless of your health. Noncancelable policies also guarantee your premiums at renewal. Guaranteed renewable policies do not.	Make sure your policy is one of these types. If it is not, you might be unable to get insurance when you need it. Make sure your policy is renewable to at least age 65. Noncancelable coverage is preferred, but may be unavailable for your occupation.
Accident AND **Illness**	Make sure benefits cover accidents *and* illnesses.
Benefit Period: The benefit period indicates the length of time the insurer must pay benefits if you become disabled. Your usual choices are *5 years*, *10 years*, *to age 65*, and *lifetime*.	Select the benefit period *to age 65* because this is about the time your retirement income should begin.

FEATURES — DISABILITY INSURANCE . . . continued	
Description	*Recommendation*
Waiting Period (or **Elimination Period**) : The waiting period indicates the length of time you must wait after becoming disabled to begin receiving benefits. Your choices are usually 30 days, 60 days, 90 days, 6 months, and 1 year.	Longer waiting periods can dramatically lower your premiums. Choose a 6 month waiting period unless you have no other form of short-term disability protection—discussed on page 21.
Any Occupation : The insurer pays the entire benefit only if you cannot perform *any* occupation. As soon as you can work at any income level, your benefits end.	Do not purchase this coverage because it does not sufficiently protect your income.
OR	
Own Occupation : The insurer pays the entire benefit if you cannot return to your specific occupation, even if you earn income from another occupation.	Do not purchase this coverage because you pay for more protection than you need.
OR	
Residual Benefits : The insurer pays the entire benefit if you cannot return to your specific occupation. However if you choose to seek other employment, your benefits are reduced by the income you earn. **Qualification Period**: The length of time you must be totally disabled before residual benefits begin.	This coverage protects your income appropriately. Make sure the policy does not require you to take the highest level of employment for which you are qualified. Request a qualification period of zero days.
OR	
Income Replacement : The insurer pays the entire benefit minus whatever you are able to earn, regardless of your occupation.	This coverage protects your income appropriately. Make sure the policy does not require you to take the highest level of employment for which you are qualified. Only a few insurers offer this coverage.
Social Security AND **Workers' Compensation Riders** : Your policy benefits are reduced by income derived from these sources. These riders lower your premiums and place the burden on your insurer to pursue benefits from these sources.	Ask for these riders because they protect your income and lower your premiums.
Automatic Benefit Increase Rider: This rider automatically increases your *COVERAGE* to keep up with inflation without requiring a medical exam.	Ask for this rider because your coverage should rise with the cost-of-living. Make sure the inflation adjustment is calculated using *compound* interest instead of *simple* interest.
OR	
Future Purchase Options (or **Guaranteed Increase Rider**) : This rider gives you the ability to periodically increase your *COVERAGE* without a medical exam.	If you expect your income to increase faster than inflation, you might want this rider instead of the *automatic benefit increase rider* just described. Make sure you don't forget to increase your coverage at the allowed times.
Cost-of-Living Rider: If you become disabled, this rider automatically increases your *BENEFITS* to keep up with inflation.	Ask for this rider because your benefits should rise with the cost-of-living. Make sure the inflation adjustment is calculated using *compound* interest instead of *simple* interest.

FEATURES — DISABILITY INSURANCE ... continued	
Description	*Recommendation*
Waiver of Premium Rider: This rider allows you to stop paying premiums while you are disabled.	Ask for this rider if your annual premium is more than a few hundred dollars.
Hospital Income Rider: This rider pays you extra income while you are in the hospital.	Do not purchase this rider because your hospital bills should be covered by your health insurance.
Return-of-Premium AND **Cash-Value Riders** : These riders allow you to bet on whether or not you will become disabled.	Do not take these costly riders.
Accidental Death and Dismemberment Rider: This rider pays a death benefit if you die in an accident.	Do not purchase this rider because it duplicates your life insurance protection.

☐ STEP 4: Choose Where to Shop

Group plans, such as those offered by unions, guilds, professional societies and alumni associations, are a good source for quality, low-cost insurance. Also, use your Yellow Pages to find phone numbers for at least ten (twenty would be better) insurance agencies that sell disability insurance.

☐ STEP 5: Shop (Do not buy or cancel any policies in this step.)

As you make your phone calls, use the shopping list on page 88 to help you describe the policies you want. Ask to receive price quotes through the mail or over the phone. If you already have privately-paid disability insurance, ask your current insurer to quote the premium for changing the policy's features to those you are shopping for.

If you find that you cannot get coverage through a private insurance company, call your state's insurance department to learn if you have other options for obtaining coverage. (Some states operate risk-sharing pools.)

☐ STEP 6: Check Insurance Company Ratings

Use the advice on page 98 to evaluate the financial strength of the insurance companies.

☐ STEP 7: Compare the Quotes

Make sure all policies are *noncancelable* or *guaranteed renewable*. (These terms are defined in the table on page 85.) Convert all monthly and semi-annual quotes to annual values so you can compare prices more easily. Find the three or four least expensive policies and ask for sample contracts. Read each contract carefully for its definition of disability and for the other rules governing your benefits. Rank your selections.

SHOPPING LIST — DISABILITY INSURANCE

	You	Spouse
Coverage	$________ per year	$________ per year
Policy Type *noncancelable term OR guaranteed renewable term*	________	________
Policy Features		
accidents AND illnesses covered	________	________
benefit period, to age 65	________	________
waiting (elimination) period, 6 months (For comparison, get quotes for 30, 60, and 90 day waiting periods too.)	________	________
residual benefits (zero qualification days) OR income replacement	________	________
benefits reduced by Social Security AND Workers' Compensation	________	________
COVERAGE (while not disabled) should increase with the cost-of-living	________	________
BENEFITS (during a disability) should increase with the cost-of-living	________	________
waiver of premium rider	________	________
	________	________

☐ STEP 8: Decide If You Will Keep Existing Policies (Do not buy or cancel any policies in this step.)

If you plan to keep a policy that provides less protection than you need, reduce the Coverage (shown above) by subtracting the coverage of the policies you will keep. Then return to STEP 5 to shop.

☐ STEP 9: Purchase the New Insurance

(Do not cancel any policies in this step.)

If the insurance company approves your application, check to see that the premium matches the original quote. If the premium has increased, do not accept the policy. Instead, ask the company to explain the increase, and then apply for coverage from several other insurers. If the companies seem to agree that you are more expensive to insure, return to STEP 7 and compare these new quotes to your existing policies.

When you purchase new coverage, reduce your premium by paying it annually instead of more frequently. If you are accustomed to paying your premium in monthly installments, be sure to budget for this annual payment.

☐ STEP 10: Cancel Your Unneeded Insurance

(Make sure your new policies are in force before cancelling any insurance.)

Read your existing policies carefully to determine *how* and *when* to cancel them. Some policies terminate automatically when you stop paying the premium, while others require a written request for cancellation. Also, some policies refund part of your premium when you cancel mid-year, while others do not. If you will not get a refund for a mid-year cancellation, wait until the end of the policy-year to cancel.

Health Insurance — Shopping Instructions

Health insurance products are difficult to compare due to their tremendous variety and complexity. If you do not have group health insurance through an employer or other group, then a major medical insurance policy is probably your most economical alternative. However, you should also see what the health maintenance organizations (HMOs) and service organizations, such as Blue Cross and Blue Shield, offer in your area.

☐ Major Medical Insurance

If you shop for major medical insurance, your deductible is usually described by three terms:

- The **deductible** is the amount you pay each year before the insurance company begins to cover expenses. Choose a *family* deductible instead of a *per person* deductible.
- Once you reach your deductible you pay a portion of the additional expenses. Your portion is called **coinsurance**. For example, if you have 80/20 coinsurance, you pay 20% of the expenses above your deductible.
- The **stop-loss** is the most you pay in a year. When your deductible and coinsurance reach the stop-loss, the insurance company pays the remainder of your covered expenses.

If you have sufficient emergency savings (discussed on page 17) you can reduce your premiums by choosing a deductible of $1,000 and a stop-loss of $5,000.

☐ Where to Shop

Group plans, such as those offered by unions, guilds, professional societies and alumni associations, may be your best source for quality, low-cost insurance. Also, phone at least ten (twenty would be better) insurance agencies listed in your Yellow Pages that sell health insurance. Ask for quotes through the mail or over the phone.

If you find that you cannot get coverage for yourself or a member of your family through a private insurance company, call your state's insurance department to learn if you have other options for obtaining coverage. (Some states operate risk-sharing pools.)

Home, Auto, & Liability Insurance — Shopping Instructions

This chapter provides step-by-step instructions to help you find quality, low-cost home, auto, and liability insurance. These policies are grouped because most insurers give a 5% to 15% discount for purchasing both home and auto insurance with them. And most insurers will not even sell you umbrella liability unless your home and auto policies are with them also.

☐ STEP 1: Describe Your Home Insurance Needs

This step will help you complete the table on page 94.

Home Description — If you already have home insurance, find your original application. It contains information you will need as you shop, such as your home's age, fire district, distance from a fire station, distance from a hydrant, and square footage. Record this information on page 94.

Dwelling — If you OWN A CONDOMINIUM, read your condominium association's insurance policy to determine where your personal coverage must begin. Make notes in the space provided on page 94. Check your current policy, or ask an insurer to help you estimate the coverage you need.

If you OWN A HOUSE OR MANUFACTURED HOME, check your current policy, or ask an insurer to help you estimate the cost to rebuild.

If you OWN AN OLDER HOME, ask an insurer to help you estimate the replacement cost of your home. If this cost is far greater than your home's market value, consider *older home* insurance as a more affordable alternative. Then ask an insurer to help you estimate your home's actual cash value.

Personal Property — Use the worksheet on the next page to estimate the cost for replacing your belongings with new ones. Enter this value on page 94. The first items on the worksheet are special because most insurers limit your protection on these. If you have a few expensive items that send you over the limits listed, do not include them on the worksheet. Instead, record them as floaters on page 94. A floater insures an item wherever it goes.

To inventory your belongings, video every item in your home. Keep appraisals and receipts for your floaters and other more valuable property. Keep these records up-to-date and safe from fire and other hazards.

Deductible — Use the information beginning on page 31 to help you select your deductible.

Liability — Use the information beginning on page 31 to help you decide how much liability and medical payments coverage to purchase. If you plan to shop for umbrella liability, write *minimum* in the blanks on page 94.

Earthquake Insurance — Decide if you want earthquake protection.

INVENTORY OF PERSONAL PROPERTY		
Category	*Replacement Cost*	*Standard Limits*
Money, gold, silver, platinum, coins, bank notes, and medals		$200
Securities, deeds, letters of credit, manuscripts, tickets, stamps, passports		$1,000
Watercraft, including their motors, trailers, furnishings, and equipment		$1,000
Trailers (not used with watercraft) and campers		$1,000
Grave markers		$1,000
Jewelry, watches, furs, and precious and semiprecious stones		*$1,000
Firearms		*$2,000
Silverware, goldware, silver-plated or gold-plated ware, and pewterware		*$2,500
Artwork		$2,500
Antiques		$2,500
Advanced electronics (cameras, computers, satellite dishes, etc.)		$2,500
Business property on premises		$2,500
Entertainment equipment (stereos, televisions, VCRs, cassettes, etc.)		
Large appliances (washer, dryer, dishwasher, refrigerator, ovens, etc.)		
Small appliances (clocks, toasters, etc.)		
Musical instruments		
Sports and hobby equipment		
Kitchen & dining ware not already listed (bowls, pots, dishes, utensils, etc.)		
Clothing		
Hygiene and cosmetic supplies		
Travel accessories		
Cleaning supplies		
Pet supplies		
Toys		
Plants and planters		
Books		
Wall hangings		
Linens		
Indoor furniture		
Outdoor furniture and grill		
Lawn and garden tools		
Other		
TOTAL Replacement Cost		

* Normally these limits apply only when items are lost by theft.

☐ STEP 2: Describe Your Auto Insurance Needs

This step will help you complete the table on page 95.

Auto Descriptions — For each car, indicate its year, make, model, and vehicle identification number (VIN). Record the mileage, and estimate the miles you drive each day. List features, such as air bags, anti-lock brakes, air conditioning, type of transmission, and type of stereo.

Liability — Use the information beginning on page 34 to help you decide how much liability coverage you need. If you plan to shop for umbrella liability, write *minimum* in the blanks on page 95.

Collision & Comprehensive, Uninsured Motorist, Underinsured Motorist, Personal Injury Protection, and Other — Use the information beginning on page 34 to help you decide how much of these coverages you need.

☐ STEP 3: Do You Want Umbrella Liability?

Use the information on page 29 to help you decide if you want umbrella liability insurance. If you do want this coverage, write the amount you want in the space beneath the words Umbrella Liability on page 96. This insurance is normally sold in million dollar increments.

☐ STEP 4: Choose Where to Shop

When you apply for a new auto policy, insurers usually check your driving record. If your record shows violations in the past three years (certain violations remain on your record longer) insurance will be more expensive. So, if your driving record includes speeding tickets or other violations, you might want to wait until your record is clear before shopping. However, your driving record should not stop you from changing the coverages of your current policy to more appropriate levels. Your current insurer is unlikely to check your record.

Consumer and financial magazines periodically evaluate insurers. Also, use your Yellow Pages to find phone numbers for at least ten (twenty would be better) insurance agencies that sell home and auto insurance.

☐ STEP 5: Shop (Do not buy or cancel any policies in this step.)

As you make your calls, pages 94 and 95 will help you describe the policies you want. Ask to receive price quotes through the mail or over the phone. Use the worksheet on page 96 to record the quotes you receive. Note whether quotes are for monthly, semi-annual, or annual premiums.

Call your current insurer(s) to learn how your premiums would change if you modified your existing policies.

If you are unable to obtain home or auto insurance through a private insurance company, call your state's insurance department to learn if you have other options for obtaining coverage. (Some states operate risk-sharing pools.)

SHOPPING LIST — HOME INSURANCE

Home Description

Dwelling

If you OWN A CONDOMINIUM

Insure to 100% of *replacement cost* ($__________) with *inflation protection* for no fewer than the standard set of 17 perils.[1]

Notes: ____

If you OWN A HOUSE OR MANUFACTURED HOME

Insure to 100% of the structure's *replacement cost* ($__________) with *inflation protection* for no fewer than the standard set of 17 perils.[1]

If you OWN AN OLDER HOME

Insure to 100% of *actual cash value* ($__________) with *inflation protection* for no fewer than the standard set of 11 perils.[1]

Personal Property

Floaters:	Item	Appraised Value
	____________________	$________
	____________________	$________
	____________________	$________
	____________________	$________
	____________________	$________
	____________________	$________

Insure your remaining possessions to their *replacement cost* of $__________.

Deductible

$__________ *(Choose a deductible of $500 or more to reduce your premiums.)*

Liability

$__________ *(Take the minimum amount of medical payments coverage allowed by the policy, usually $1,000.)*

Earthquake Insurance

Do you want this coverage? *YES* *NO*

---

[1] The first 11 perils include fire & lightning, windstorm & hail, explosion, riots, aircraft, vehicles, smoke, vandalism, theft, glass breakage, and volcanic eruption. The remaining 6 include falling objects, weight of ice, snow & sleet, and damage to plumbing, heating, air conditioning, electrical wiring & appliances due to ice, water, steam & electrical current.

SHOPPING LIST — AUTO INSURANCE

Auto Descriptions

	Auto 1	Auto 2	Auto 3	Auto 4
year:	________	________	________	________
make:	________	________	________	________
model:	________	________	________	________
VIN:	________	________	________	________
	________	________	________	________
mileage:	________	________	________	________
daily miles:	________	________	________	________
features:	________	________	________	________
	________	________	________	________
	________	________	________	________
	________	________	________	________
	________	________	________	________

Liability bodily injury—BI: $_______ per person $_______ per accident *(set by insurer)*

property damage—PD: $_______ per accident

Collision & Comprehensive *(recommended if vehicle is valued at more than $2,000)*

	Auto 1	Auto 2	Auto 3	Auto 4
Carry this coverage?	YES NO	YES NO	YES NO	YES NO
Deductible *($500 or more)*:	$______	$______	$______	$______

UNinsured Motorist BI: $_______ *(minimum)* per person $_______ *(minimum)* per accident

PD: $_______ *(minimum)* per accident

UNDERinsured Motorist BI: $_______ *($0)* per person $_______ *($0)* per accident

PD: $_______ *($0)* per accident

Personal Injury Protection PIP: __________ *(minimum)* deductible: __________ *(maximum)*

Other Coverages *(not recommended)*

SHOPPING WORKSHEET				
Insurance Company company name phone number agent's name	**Home** annual premium	**Auto** annual premium	**Umbrella Liability** $__________ annual premium	**TOTAL** annual premium with multiple policy discounts

☐ STEP 6: Compare the Quotes

Convert all monthly and semi-annual quotes to annual values so you can compare the policies easily. Select and rank your top three choices.

☐ STEP 7: Check Insurance Company Ratings

Use the advice on page 98 to help you evaluate the financial strength of each insurance company.

☐ STEP 8: Purchase the New Insurance

(Do not cancel any policies in this step.)

If the insurance company approves your applications, check to see that the premiums match the original quotes. If the premiums are higher, do not accept the policies. Instead, ask the company to explain the increases, and then apply for coverage from several other insurers. If the companies seem to agree that you are more expensive to insure, return to STEP 6 and compare these new quotes to your existing policies. It may be cheaper to keep your current coverage.

When you purchase new coverage, reduce your premiums by paying them annually instead of more frequently. If you are accustomed to paying your premiums in monthly installments, be sure to budget for these annual payments.

☐ STEP 9: Cancel Your Unneeded Insurance

(Make sure your new policies are in force before cancelling any insurance.)

Insurance Company Ratings

There are several services that rate the financial strength of insurance companies:

- A.M. Best Company
- Duff & Phelps Credit Rating Company
- Moody's Investors Service
- Standard & Poor's Corporation
- Weiss Research

You can obtain ratings from your insurance agent (or quote service), your state's insurance department, your local library, or the ratings firms directly.

Each ratings service uses a different grading scheme. Avoid insurance companies with ratings below the lines shown in the following table.

INSURANCE COMPANY RATINGS

Best	*D&P*	*Moody's*	*S&P*	*Weiss*
A++	AAA	Aaa	AAA	A+
A+	AA+	Aa1	AA+	A
A	AA	Aa2	AA	A-
A-	AA-	Aa3	AA-	B+
B++	A+	A1	A+	B
B+	A	A2	A	B-
B	A-	A3	A-	C+
B-	BBB+	Baa1	BBB+	C
C++	BBB	Baa2	BBB	C-
C+	BBB-	Baa3	BBB-	D+
C	BB+	Ba1	BB+	D
C-	BB	Ba2	BB	D-
D	BB-	Ba3	BB-	E+
E	B+	B1	B+	E
F	B	B2	B	F
	B-	B3	B-	
	CCC+	Caa	CCC	
	CCC	Ca	R	
	CCC-	C		

Mutual Funds

What Are They?....................................99
How Money Grows..............................100
Understanding Risk..............................100
How To Choose Funds..........................101
How To Buy Fund Shares......................102
Costs...103
Where To Shop..................................103

☐ What Are They?

Mutual funds help small investors participate in the stock and bond markets. Each fund pools the savings of many small investors to make one large investor . . . and a large investor has many advantages over a smaller one.

Investing in a mutual fund is like buying stock in a company—your dollars buy shares of the mutual fund, and the value of these shares can fluctuate from day-to-day. The primary difference between a mutual fund and a stock is that a mutual fund's share does not represent ownership of a single company, but instead represents ownership of many companies, or bonds, or other types of securities.

Mutual funds offer:

- **Diversification**
  Diversification reduces your risk. Consider a mutual fund that owns stock in 50 different companies. If one of these companies goes bankrupt, the value of the mutual fund falls, but only a little because there are still 49 other companies. A mutual fund protects you by spreading your money among many investments. For small investors, such diversification is expensive or impossible without mutual funds.
- **Professional Management**
  Mutual funds are managed by people who specialize in making investment decisions.
- **Convenience**
  Mutual funds do your record-keeping. You receive statements of your account activity and performance. You also receive information to help you do your taxes. Mutual funds give you quick access to your money. A toll-free phone call is usually all it takes to move or withdraw money. And some funds offer free checking, however limits are usually placed on the size and number of checks you may write.
- **Protection**
  A mutual fund's underlying securities must be held by an independent custodian, usually a bank. This means that your investments cannot be seized if your fund company goes bankrupt. Also, a mutual fund must maintain minimum standards for diversification to ensure that your

investment dollars are spread. **NOTE: Money placed in mutual funds is not insured like it is in a bank.** (There are, however, funds that invest exclusively in government insured securities.)

- **Variety**
  There are mutual funds for just about every investment strategy.

☐ How Money Grows

Money grows in two ways—income and capital appreciation. **Income** results when bonds pay interest or stocks pay dividends. **Capital appreciation** results when your investments become more valuable than the amount you paid for them.

There is also one way for money to shrink. **Capital depreciation** occurs when your investments become less valuable than the amount you paid for them.

☐ Understanding Risk

In general, the faster you try to make your money grow, the greater your risk of capital depreciation. Here are the types of risk you face.

- **Investment Risk**: The value of a mutual fund depends on the financial strength of the firms or governments it invests in. You can somewhat control your exposure to this risk with the types of mutual funds you choose—for instance, high yield "junk" bond funds versus government insured bond funds.
- **Market Risk**: The value of a mutual fund may rise and fall with the overall market, regardless of the financial strength of its underlying holdings. Stick to your investment plan. Don't move in and out of funds in reaction to price swings.
- **Currency Risk**: The performance of a mutual fund that invests abroad depends partly on currency exchange rates. As these rates change unpredictably, they can dramatically enhance or erode your fund's performance. To insulate yourself from currency risk and still participate in world markets, put most of your long-term savings in funds that invest domestically, because many U.S. firms are themselves globally invested.
- **Political Risk**: The performance of a mutual fund that invests abroad depends on the political stability of the home countries. Political risk (like currency risk) presents another compelling reason to participate in global markets primarily through funds that invest domestically.
- **Interest Rate Risk (bond funds only)**: This risk is greater than many people realize. The share price of a mutual fund that invests in bonds depends on interest rates. As interest rates rise, bond fund prices fall. Here's an example to illustrate why (using a single bond instead of a bond fund). Assume you buy a new bond for $100 that pays you 5% interest. One year later, interest rates have climbed to 10% and you decide to sell your bond. Can you get your $100 back? The answer comes from the buyer who can purchase a new bond for $100 paying 10%, or purchase your bond for $100 paying 5%. If you were the buyer, what would you do? In order for you to sell your bond, you will have to lower your price.

How To Choose Funds

Mutual funds fall into four broad categories:

- **Stock Funds** range from those that seek dividend income only, to those that seek capital appreciation only. All have share prices that fluctuate.
- **Bond Funds**[1] seek interest income only. All have share prices that fluctuate except for **money market funds**.
- **Balanced Funds** invest in a mix of both stocks and bonds. All have share prices that fluctuate.
- **Asset Allocation Funds** invest in a flexible mix of stocks and/or bonds. The mix changes in anticipation of market and economic developments. All have share prices that fluctuate.

Within each fund category there are many mutual funds. Ask your mutual fund company to help you identify specific funds suited to your investment goals, risk tolerance, and tax bracket. (Page 103 will help you shop for a mutual fund company.) The following two tables summarize stock and bond fund types. Balanced funds and asset allocation funds are not mentioned in the tables because these funds combine attributes of both stock and bond funds.

[1] For this discussion, the term *bond* includes debt securities such as treasury bills, treasury notes, and commercial paper that are not officially called bonds.

STOCK FUND TYPES

Equity Income Funds invest in established companies that pay above average dividends.

Growth & Income Funds invest in companies that pay dividends and that also exhibit the potential for larger dividends and capital appreciation. Share prices tend to be less stable than those for equity income funds.

Growth Funds invest in companies with potential for large capital appreciation. They pay few dividends. Share prices tend to be less stable than those for growth & income funds.

Aggressive Growth Funds strive for maximum capital appreciation. They typically invest in emerging companies and industries. They pay few dividends, and share prices tend to be less stable than those for growth funds.

Sector Funds invest in companies in a particular industry. Share prices tend to be less stable than those for funds that invest in companies across many industries.

Small Company Funds invest in small companies with potential for large capital appreciation. They pay few dividends. Share prices tend to be less stable than those for funds that invest in companies of many sizes.

Nation Funds invest in companies from a single country.

International Funds invest in companies from several countries.

Index Funds invest in those companies used to measure market performance, such as the S&P 500 or the Wilshire 4500. These funds have low management fees because they do not research companies. They simply invest in the stocks that comprise the index.

BOND FUND TYPES

Money Market Funds invest in bonds with maturities averaging around 90 days. Share prices do not fluctuate. These funds usually pay more interest than a savings account but less than other bond funds. They are the safest type of mutual fund because they maintain a constant share price of $1, so there is no capital appreciation or depreciation. The $1 share price is not guaranteed, but since 1972 (the year these funds were created) it has never changed. When you invest in Money Market Funds, go with a large mutual fund company. If the market pressures the share price to fall, a larger company will probably bail you out to maintain investor confidence. (Numerous such bailouts have already occurred.)

Short-Term Funds invest in bonds with maturities averaging around 3 years. Share prices fluctuate. These funds usually pay more interest than money market funds.

Intermediate-Term Funds invest in bonds with maturities averaging around 10 years. Share prices tend to be less stable than those for short-term funds, but intermediate-term funds usually pay more interest.

Long-Term Funds invest in bonds with maturities averaging around 20 years. Share prices tend to be less stable than those for intermediate-term funds, but long-term funds usually pay more interest.

Municipal Funds invest in bonds backed by state and local governments. Interest is exempt from federal taxes and may be exempt from state and local taxes if the securities are from your home state. They tend to pay less interest than fully taxable funds, but this lost interest may be more than offset by tax savings, depending on your tax bracket. Your mutual fund company can help you compare these funds to fully taxable funds. **Municipal funds are inappropriate for retirement savings that are already exempt from taxes.**

U.S. Treasury Funds invest in treasury securities backed by the federal government. Interest is exempt from state and local taxes, but not federal taxes. They tend to pay less interest than fully taxable funds, but this lost interest may be more than offset by tax savings, depending on your tax bracket. Your mutual fund company can help you compare these funds to fully taxable funds. **U.S. Treasury funds are inappropriate for retirement savings that are already exempt from taxes.**

Government Insured Funds invest in bonds backed by the federal government. Interest is fully taxable.

Corporate Funds invest in debt securities of businesses. Interest is fully taxable.

High Yield Funds invest in lower quality securities, sometimes called *junk bonds*. These funds pay high interest because of the greater risk that some of the companies issuing the bonds will default.

Nation Funds invest in bonds from a single country.

International Funds invest in bonds from several countries.

Index Funds invest in those bonds used to measure market performance, such as the Bond Buyer 40 or Lehman Brothers. These funds have low management fees because they do not research bond issuers. They simply invest in the securities that comprise the index.

☐ How To Buy Fund Shares

Share prices fluctuate for all but money market funds. For those that fluctuate, you want to buy shares when their prices are lowest. This is called *timing the market*. It is difficult to do, even for the experts. Fortunately, there is a simple technique for helping you buy at low prices. The technique involves making regular purchases regardless of the market's position. Consider the following example. You invest $120 per month for three months. Shares cost $10 the first month, $8 the second month, and $6 the third month. What is the average price you paid for your shares? The answer appears to be $8, but this is incorrect. You actually paid less because your $120 bought 12 shares the first month, 15 shares the second month, and 20 shares the third month. You spent a total of $360 for 47 shares, making your average share price $7.66. This technique is called **dollar cost averaging**, and it helps you buy more shares when prices are lower.

If you want to try playing the market, here are some tips:

- Subscribe to an investment newsletter for advice about *what* and *when* to buy and sell. A subscription costs a few hundred dollars per year, but good advice pays for itself quickly. Find the latest edition of *The Hulbert Guide to Financial Newsletters* for help choosing a newsletter.
- Save money by using a discount broker. This type of broker simply executes your trades without giving advice. Many mutual fund companies offer convenient discount brokerage services.
- For optimum performance, only play the market with money held in tax-deferred accounts, such as IRAs or other retirement plans. This strategy allows your money to grow much faster because it postpones the tax consequences of selling securities for a profit.

□ Costs

All mutual funds charge an annual management fee ranging from 1/4% to more than 1% of your money. If this is the only fee, the fund is called *no-load.* If you are charged any of the following additional fees, the fund is called *loaded.*

- **Front-End Loads** (or **Sales Charges**) pay commissions when you invest. These charges can be as much as 8 1/2% of your money.
- **Back-End Loads** (or **Contingent Deferred Sales Charges**) penalize you for withdrawals during the first five or six years. These charges can be as much as 6% for money withdrawn in the first year, usually declining by 1% each year thereafter.
- **Dividend Reinvestment Fees** are charges on your reinvested earnings.
- **Fixed Redemption Charges** (or **Exit Fees**) are paid to the mutual fund company when you withdraw money, regardless of how long your money has been invested.
- **12b-1 Fees** are annual charges that pay for advertising, fund literature, and other marketing costs. This fee ranges from 1/4% to 1 1/4% of your money.

Does money grow fast enough in loaded funds to justify the additional fees? The answer appears to be no. In fact, the evidence suggests that the average no-load fund performs better than the average loaded fund. Stick to no-load funds unless the track record of your loaded fund suggests that it will perform well enough to justify its fees.

□ Where To Shop

Your best value is to buy mutual funds directly from the companies that sell them. Simply call a mutual fund company and ask to receive a summary of its funds and an application. For a complete listing of mutual fund companies and the funds they offer, refer to consumer and financial magazines at your local library.

For your convenience, phone numbers are provided for several large and reputable mutual fund companies. Each company has a history of good performance and good customer service. Each company offers a wide variety of funds—all of which are no-load. And each company supports IRAs, Uniform Gift-Transfer to Minor Accounts, and more.

20th Century	800-345-2021	T. Rowe Price	800-638-5660
Scudder	800-225-2470	Vanguard	800-662-7447
Stein Roe	800-338-2550		

You can also buy mutual funds through sales people such as bankers, brokers, and financial planners. However, you pay for this personalized service. (Mutual funds are not federally insured, even when sold through a bank.)

ANNUITIES

What Are They? 105
Annuity Types 105
Costs 105
Where To Shop 106
What To Do With An Annuity You Don't Need 106

☐ What Are They?

Annuities are tax-deferred investments designed for retirement savings. They can be good investments if you need more retirement savings than your employer plan and IRA allow. However, they should not be used for savings you will need prior to age 59 1/2, because the federal government levies a 10% penalty (and your state might also levy a penalty) on the tax-deferred portion of early withdrawals.

Annuities give you two options at retirement: you may withdraw your money as you like, or you may *annuitize* your account. *Annuitizing* means you are guaranteed an income for life. When you annuitize, you gamble that you will live beyond your life expectancy. Because of this gamble, annuities must be sold by insurance companies.

☐ Annuity Types

There are two types of annuity—fixed and variable. A **fixed annuity** guarantees you a specific return on your money. A **variable annuity** does not guarantee your return, but instead provides you with the ability to invest conservatively or aggressively, usually in mutual funds.

Avoid fixed annuities because your money is mingled with the insurance company's. If the insurer goes bankrupt, your protection is limited to the coverage offered by your state's reserve system (if it has one). Variable annuities do not pose this danger because the law requires your investments to be held by a trustee, separate from the insurance company. Furthermore, your money has more growth potential in a variable annuity because you can invest in stock mutual funds.

☐ Costs

There are four costs to consider when comparing **variable annuities** that invest in mutual funds.

- **Mutual Fund Fees** are described on page 103. Choose an annuity that invests in no-load mutual funds.

- **Withdrawal Penalties** may be imposed if you withdraw more than a certain percentage of your annuity in a single year. Penalties may also be imposed if you withdraw money during the first few years of your annuity. Choose an annuity with no withdrawal penalties.
- **Expense and Mortality Fees** pay initial sales commissions, annuity set-up costs, and death benefits. The fee is a percentage of your annuity's value—usually around 1%.
- **Contract Maintenance Charges** pay the insurance company for managing your investments. This charge is typically a flat fee ranging from $25 to $50 per year.

☐ Where To Shop

The best variable annuities are sold through mutual fund companies. Ask your favorite fund company if they offer annuities. Ask to receive information and an application. Make sure the annuity you choose gives you the flexibility to vary and completely stop your contributions. This flexibility lets you shift your annuity contributions to an employer retirement plan or IRA if larger tax-deductible contributions become allowed.

A more costly alternative is to buy annuities through sales people such as bankers, brokers, financial planners, and insurance agents. (Annuities are not federally insured, even when sold through a bank.)

☐ What To Do With An Annuity You Don't Need

If you own an annuity you don't need, you have several options. Read your contract carefully before you act.

Option A: Cancel the annuity and collect the proceeds.
Do not consider this option, because the federal government levies a 10% penalty on the tax-deferred portion of withdrawals made before age $59^1/_2$ (your state may also levy a penalty). Also, you must pay income taxes on the tax-deferred earnings, and the insurance company may charge you a withdrawal penalty.

Option B: Keep the annuity and continue your contributions as scheduled.
Do not consider this option, because your contributions to an annuity are not tax-deductible. Therefore, you would be better-off contributing this money to an employer plan or IRA instead.

Option C: Keep the annuity, but stop making contributions.
Consider this option if your policy lets you stop making payments and you cannot find a better annuity in Option D.

Option D: Exchange your annuity for a better one.
Consider this option if you can find an annuity where lower costs and greater investment growth should offset your withdrawal penalty. You can easily avoid government penalties and taxes by having the new insurance company handle the exchange for you. If your current insurer is highly rated (see page 98) and offers a better annuity than the one you already have, see if the company will waive its withdrawal penalty for an in-house exchange.

INDEX

12b-1 fees (mutual funds), 103
401(k)s, 6
403(b)s, 6

A

A.M. Best Company, 98
accidental death and dismemberment rider (disability insurance), 87
accidental death rider (life insurance), 78
actual cash value (home insurance), 31-32
adjustable life insurance, 77
  see also cash-value life insurance
aggressive growth stock funds, 101
annual renewable term life insurance, 77
annuities, 105
  for retirement savings, 8
  for college savings, 16
any occupation (disability insurance), 86
asset allocation funds, 101
auto insurance, 34
  when renting a car, truck, or trailer, 37
  shopping instructions, 91
automatic benefit increase rider (disability insurance), 86
automatic withdrawal, 8

B

back-end loads (mutual funds), 103
balanced funds, 101
Barron's Complete College Financing Guide, 14
benefit period (disability insurance), 85
bodily injury liability (auto insurance), 35
bond funds, 101
budgeting, 42

C

capital appreciation, 100
capital depreciation, 100
cash-value life insurance, 77
  for retirement savings, 9
  for college savings, 16
  for estate planning, 5
  options for cancelling, 80
cash-value rider (disability insurance), 87
Certified Financial Planners (CFPs), 47
children's protection rider (life insurance), 78
coinsurance (health insurance), 90
College Handbook, The, 12, 45
college savings, 12
CollegeSure CD, 15
collision (auto insurance), 34-35
commission-only financial planners, 47
comprehensive (auto insurance), 34-35
Consumer Federation of America, 81
contingent deferred sales charges (mutual funds), 103
contract maintenance charges (annuities), 106
convertibility rider (life insurance), 78
corporate bond funds
cost-of-living rider
  life insurance, 78
  disability insurance, 86
currency risk, 100

D

damage waiver (auto insurance), 37
deductibles
  health insurance, 90
  home insurance, 31-32
  auto insurance, 34, 36
deferred compensation, 6
dental insurance, 27
disability insurance
  short-term, 21
  long-term, 22
  shopping instructions, 85
discount broker, 103
dismemberment (auto insurance), 36
diversification, 99
dividend reinvestment fees (mutual funds), 103
dollar cost averaging, 103
double indemnity (life insurance), 78
Duff & Phelps Credit Rating Company, 98
dwelling (home insurance), 31-32

E

earthquake insurance, 33
elimination period (disability insurance), 86
emergency savings, 17
employer benefits
  retirement plans, 6
  life insurance, 18
  sick leave, 21
  disability insurance, 21-23
  group health insurance, 27
equity income stock funds, 101

estate planning
for severe disability, 38
for death, 39
cash-value life insurance, 5
stock mutual funds, 5
exit fees (mutual funds), 103
expense and mortality fees (annuities), 106

F

fee-based financial planners, 47
fee-only financial planners, 47
Fidelity *Thinkware*
ordering information, 5
for retirement planning, 54
for life insurance planning, 68
financial planners, 47
fixed annuities, 105
fixed redemption charges (mutual funds), 103
flood insurance, 33
front-end loads (mutual funds), 103
future purchase options (disability insurance), 86

G

government insured bond funds, 102
gross income, 50
group health insurance, 27
growth & income stock funds, 101
growth stock funds, 101
guaranteed increase rider (disability insurance), 86
guaranteed insurability rider (life insurance), 78
guaranteed rates (life insurance), 79
guaranteed renewable (disability insurance), 85

H

health insurance, 27
health maintenance organizations (HMOs), 90
high yield bond funds
home insurance, 31
standard exclusions, 33
shopping instructions, 91
hospital income rider (disability insurance), 87
Hulbert Guide to Financial Newsletters, The, 103

I

income replacement (disability insurance), 86
index bond funds, 102
index stock funds, 101
individual retirement accounts (IRAs), 8
inflation protection (home insurance), 31-32
Institute of Certified Financial Planners, 47
insurance company ratings, 98
InsuranceQuote, 78
interest rate risk, 100
intermediate-term bond funds, 102
international bond funds, 102
international stock funds, 101
investment risk, 100
irrevocable trusts, 40 (footnote)

J

Jack White & Co., 78

K

Keoghs, 6

L

laws & ordinances, 33
level premium disability insurance, 85
level premium term life insurance, 77
liability insurance, 29
home insurance, 31-32
auto insurance, 34-35
umbrella liability, 30
shopping instructions, 91
liability insurance supplement (auto insurance), 37
life insurance, 18
for children, 19
during retirement, 20
estimating your needs, 59
shopping instructions, 76
managing benefits, 82
LifeQuote, 78
LifeRates, 78
living trusts, 40 (footnote)
living will, 38
loaded mutual funds, 103
long-term bond funds, 102
loss of sight (auto insurance), 36

M

major medical insurance, 90
Make Your Own Living Trust, 41
market risk, 100
market timing, 102-103
MasterQuote, 78
maternity insurance, 27
Medicaid, 27
medical payments (auto insurance), 36

medical payments to others (home insurance), 31-32
Medicare, 27
money market funds, 101-102
Moody's Investors Service, 98
mortgage insurance, 80
municipal bond funds, 102
mutual funds, 99

N

nation bond funds, 102
nation stock funds, 101
National Association of Personal Financial Advisors (NAPFA), 47
National Flood Insurance Program, 33
net income, 50
net worth, 51
no-load mutual funds, 103
Nolo's Simple Will Book, 41
noncancelable (disability insurance), 85

O

ordinary life insurance, 77
  see also cash-value life insurance
own occupation (disability insurance), 86

P

payroll deduction, 8
pensions, 6
Personal Earnings and Benefit Estimate Statement, 52
personal injury protection (PIP) (auto insurance), 34, 36
personal property (home insurance), 31-32
political risk, 100
power of attorney, 38
Power of Attorney Book, The, 38
prepaid tuition programs, 16
prescription drug insurance, 27
probate, 40
profit-sharing, 6
property damage liability (auto insurance), 35

Q

qualification period (disability insurance), 86
Quicken Family Lawyer, 41
Quotesmith, 78

R

re-entry (life insurance), 78
renewable (life insurance), 77
renewable term disability insurance, 85
rental reimbursement (auto insurance), 36
renting a car, truck, or trailer (auto insurance), 37
replacement cost (home insurance), 31-32
residual benefits (disability insurance), 86
retirement savings, 4, 54
return-of-premium rider (disability insurance), 87
revocable trusts, 40 (footnote)
risk sharing pools
  life insurance, 18
  disability insurance, 22
  health insurance, 27
  home and auto insurance, 93
road service (auto insurance), 36
rollover IRA, 6

S

sales charges (mutual funds), 103
savings bonds, 14-15
Scudder Mutual Funds, 104
sector stock funds, 101
SelectQuote, 78
short-term bond funds, 102
simplified employee pensions (SEPs), 6
single-limit liability (auto insurance), 35
single premium life insurance, 77
  see also cash-value life insurance
small company stock funds, 101
Social Security
  estimating your benefits, 52
  life insurance, 18
  disability insurance, 23-24
Social Security rider (disability insurance), 86
split-limit liability (auto insurance), 35
Standard & Poor's Corporation, 98
state education bonds, 14
Stein Roe Mutual Funds, 104
stock funds, 101
  for retirement savings, 10
  for college savings, 13
  for estate planning, 5
stop-loss (health insurance), 90
supplemental accident insurance, 28
systematic withdrawals, 82-83

T

T. Rowe Price Mutual Funds, 104
T. Rowe Price *Retirement Planning Kit*
  ordering information, 5
  for retirement planning, 57
  for life insurance planning, 70
tax-free *versus* taxable return, 14
tax-sheltered annuities (TSAs), 6

The 10% Rule (retirement savings), 4
term life insurance, 77
TermQuote, 78
timing the market, 102-103
trusts, 39-40
20th Century Mutual Funds, 104

U

umbrella liability insurance, 30
underinsured motorist (auto insurance), 36
Uniform Gift-Transfer to Minor Accounts, 14
uninsured motorist (auto insurance), 34, 36
universal life insurance, 77
  see also cash-value life insurance
U.S. treasury bond funds

V

Vanguard Mutual Funds, 104
variable annuities, 105
variable life insurance, 77
  see also cash-value life insurance
variable universal life insurance, 77
  see also cash-value life insurance
Veterans' benefits
  life insurance, 18
  disability insurance, 21, 23-24
  health insurance, 27

W

waiting period (disability insurance), 86
waiver of premium rider
  life insurance, 78
  disability insurance, 87
Weiss Research, 98
whole life insurance, 77
  see also cash-value life insurance
wills, 39
withdrawal penalties (annuities), 106
Workers' Compensation
  life insurance, 18
  disability insurance, 21, 23-24
  health insurance, 27
Workers' Compensation rider (disability insurance), 86

BOOK ORDER FORM

Please send _____ book(s) to . . .
number

Name ______________________________

Address ______________________________

____

City ______________________________

State __________ Zip Code _____________

$14.95 per book

Free delivery

When shipped to a Wisconsin address, please add 5.5% sales tax.

Make your check payable to Financial Sense.

Mail your order to: Financial Sense
3818 Birch Avenue
Madison, WI 53711

BOOK ORDER FORM

Please send _____ book(s) to . . .
number

Name ______________________________

Address ______________________________

____

City ______________________________

State __________ Zip Code _____________

$14.95 per book

Free delivery

When shipped to a Wisconsin address, please add 5.5% sales tax.

Make your check payable to Financial Sense.

Mail your order to: Financial Sense
3818 Birch Avenue
Madison, WI 53711

BOOK ORDER FORM

Please send _____ book(s) to . . .
number

Name ______________________________

Address ______________________________

____

City ______________________________

State __________ Zip Code _____________

$14.95 per book

Free delivery

When shipped to a Wisconsin address, please add 5.5% sales tax.

Make your check payable to Financial Sense.

Mail your order to: Financial Sense
3818 Birch Avenue
Madison, WI 53711

BOOK ORDER FORM

Please send _____ book(s) to . . .
number

Name ______________________________

Address ______________________________

____

City ______________________________

State _________ Zip Code ____________

$14.95 per book

Free delivery

When shipped to a Wisconsin address, please add 5.5% sales tax.

Make your check payable to Financial Sense.

Mail your order to: Financial Sense
3818 Birch Avenue
Madison, WI 53711

BOOK ORDER FORM

Please send _____ book(s) to . . .
number

Name ______________________________

Address ______________________________

____

City ______________________________

State _________ Zip Code ____________

$14.95 per book

Free delivery

When shipped to a Wisconsin address, please add 5.5% sales tax.

Make your check payable to Financial Sense.

Mail your order to: Financial Sense
3818 Birch Avenue
Madison, WI 53711

BOOK ORDER FORM

Please send _____ book(s) to . . .
number

Name ______________________________

Address ______________________________

____

City ______________________________

State _________ Zip Code ____________

$14.95 per book

Free delivery

When shipped to a Wisconsin address, please add 5.5% sales tax.

Make your check payable to Financial Sense.

Mail your order to: Financial Sense
3818 Birch Avenue
Madison, WI 53711

BOOK ORDER FORM

Please send _____ book(s) to . . . (number) Name ____________________ Address ____________________ ____________________ City ____________________ State ________ Zip Code ________	$14.95 per book Free delivery When shipped to a Wisconsin address, please add 5.5% sales tax. Make your check payable to Financial Sense. Mail your order to: Financial Sense 3818 Birch Avenue Madison, WI 53711

BOOK ORDER FORM

Please send _____ book(s) to . . . (number) Name ____________________ Address ____________________ ____________________ City ____________________ State ________ Zip Code ________	$14.95 per book Free delivery When shipped to a Wisconsin address, please add 5.5% sales tax. Make your check payable to Financial Sense. Mail your order to: Financial Sense 3818 Birch Avenue Madison, WI 53711

BOOK ORDER FORM

Please send _____ book(s) to . . . (number) Name ____________________ Address ____________________ ____________________ City ____________________ State ________ Zip Code ________	$14.95 per book Free delivery When shipped to a Wisconsin address, please add 5.5% sales tax. Make your check payable to Financial Sense. Mail your order to: Financial Sense 3818 Birch Avenue Madison, WI 53711